COORDINATION
COLLABORATION
CAPACITY

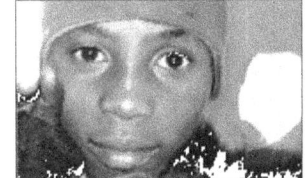

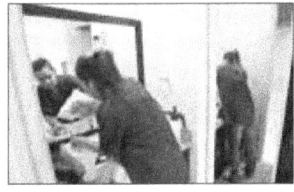

Federal Strategic Action Plan
on Services for Victims of Human Trafficking
in the United States
2013-2017

"We will invest in helping trafficking victims rebuild their lives."

– President Barack Obama, December 31, 2012

COORDINATION, COLLABORATION, CAPACITY

Federal Strategic Action Plan
on Services for Victims of Human Trafficking
in the United States
2013-2017

CO-CHAIRS OF PLANNING PROCESS

Department of Justice (DOJ)
Department of Health and Human Services (HHS)
Department of Homeland Security (DHS)

PRESIDENT'S INTERAGENCY TASK FORCE
TO MONITOR AND COMBAT TRAFFICKING IN PERSONS

Department of State (DOS)
Department of Defense (DOD)
Department of Justice (DOJ)
Department of the Interior (DOI)
Department of Agriculture (USDA)
Department of Labor (DOL)
Department of Health and Human Services (HHS)
Department of Transportation (DOT)
Department of Education (ED)
Department of Homeland Security (DHS)
Domestic Policy Council (DPC)
National Security Staff (NSS)
Office of Management and Budget (OMB)
Office of the Director of National Intelligence (ODNI)
Federal Bureau of Investigation (FBI)
U.S. Agency for International Development (USAID)
U.S. Equal Employment Opportunity Commission (EEOC)

Human trafficking is a denial of our common humanity and an affront to our ideals as Americans. My Administration is committed to combating this modern incarnation of slavery. That is why I am proud to release the *Federal Strategic Action Plan on Services for Victims of Human Trafficking in the United States 2013-2017*, a collaborative effort involving more than 15 agencies across the Federal Government.

Survivors of human trafficking have had their lives ripped apart, and they deserve holistic, streamlined, and compassionate assistance as they rebuild their lives and their futures. This Plan's victim-centered approach is necessary to effectively meet the needs of survivors, whether they have been trapped in a home as a domestic worker, brought to the United States as a migrant laborer under false pretenses, or forced to engage in commercial sex acts. While the work to combat human trafficking and assist victims has been tremendous, there is more to be done. This Plan is part of my commitment that more *will* be done.

Human trafficking is insidious and widespread, so we have forged partnerships across the Federal Government, and with survivors; private entities; state, local, and tribal governments; non-profit organizations; philanthropies; and the faith community, to expand our efforts and reach as many survivors as we can.

To those who are suffering and have suffered the horrors of human trafficking, our message remains: We hear you. We insist on your dignity. And we share your belief, that if just given the chance, you can forge a life equal to your talents and worthy of your dreams.

Sincerely,

Dear Reader:

Human trafficking is a crime that strikes at the very heart of the American promise: freedom. In response to this abhorrent crime, government agencies and nongovernmental organizations have formed strong and growing partnerships aimed at ending this violation of fundamental civil rights and human dignity.

We are honored to co-chair the first *Federal Strategic Action Plan on Services for Victims of Human Trafficking in the United States 2013–2017* (Plan), which lays out a 5-year path for further strengthening coordination, collaboration, and capacity across governmental and nongovernmental entities dedicated to providing support to the victims of human trafficking. The Obama Administration is providing unparalleled leadership to address this crime. The President's request for an interagency plan to strengthen services to trafficking victims demonstrates the Administration's commitment to anti-human trafficking efforts and reaffirms federal responsibility to support the victims of human trafficking. With guidance from the President's Interagency Task Force to Monitor and Combat Trafficking in Persons, we worked

across agencies to develop a plan for victim services that provides a roadmap for aligning federal efforts to aid victims, improve understanding among federal and nonfederal entities who work to support victims, expand victim access to services, and improve outcomes for survivors of human trafficking. We partnered with government and nongovernmental stakeholders across the country through the receipt and careful consideration of public comments on the draft strategic action plan, and by conducting listening sessions and community meetings. Creating the Plan was an energizing process that brought together experts in the field and fostered the development of innovative strategies and solutions.

In developing the Plan, our agencies were able to draw on long experience in protecting and supporting victims of human trafficking. For example, the Department of Health and Human Services has supported extensive outreach efforts aimed at trafficking victims, built community capacity to address human trafficking through local coalitions, and supported services to hundreds of victims through grants, contracts, and certifications for foreign national victims. The Department of Homeland Security has integrated the identification of human trafficking perpetrators and victims into its operations and implemented critical immigration protections for victims and penalties for traffickers. The Department of Justice has supported the development of multidisciplinary task forces across the United States to investigate and prosecute traffickers, support victims, and educate the public; and provided funding to victim-serving organizations that work to ensure that all victims have access to the comprehensive services they need to rebuild their lives. In addition, our federal, state, local, tribal, and territorial partners continue to demonstrate commitment and leadership through ongoing and increasing participation in interagency discussions and initiatives on victim services.

The Plan will remain a living document. We will revisit and refine the Plan as promising practices emerge and as we identify additional opportunities for coordination. We anticipate future expansion of the Plan to reflect enhanced government partnerships with the nonprofit, public, and private sectors and strengthened holistic responses to the needs of victims of all forms of human trafficking.

We look forward to the work ahead.

Sincerely,

Eric H. Holder, Jr.
Attorney General

Kathleen Sebelius
*Secretary of Health
and Human Services*

Jeh Charles Johnson
*Secretary of
Homeland Security*

Commitment to Action

PRESIDENT'S INTERAGENCY TASK FORCE TO MONITOR AND COMBAT TRAFFICKING IN PERSONS

Human trafficking, also known as trafficking in persons or modern day slavery, is an affront to the most basic of human freedoms. To combat this unspeakable crime and protect its victims, we build on more than a decade of progress in developing services and support networks that provide survivors of human trafficking with a path to freedom, independence, and self-sufficiency. We recognize that services must be provided in a manner that respects survivors and endeavors to integrate their experience and their voice.

As members of the President's Interagency Task Force to Monitor and Combat Trafficking in Persons, we commit ourselves anew to a holistic and comprehensive victim-centered approach, one that is meaningfully informed by survivor input and accompanied by well-coordinated and effective public awareness and outreach efforts designed to identify victims and prevent anyone from ever becoming a victim of this crime that tears at the social fabric of our Nation.

We will uphold a system that recognizes all victims of human trafficking—whether adults or children, male, female, or transgender individuals, U.S. citizens or noncitizens—regardless of the type of modern day slavery they endured.

We will build new partnerships and collaborate with international, federal, state, territorial, tribal, and local counterparts, the private sector, and nongovernmental organizations and advocates to amplify our efforts and multiply our forces.

As the President's Interagency Task Force to Monitor and Combat Trafficking in Persons, we will work tirelessly to fulfill the commitments set forth above and continuously evaluate our efforts and adapt our goals as needed to ensure the most effective U.S. Government response.

Department of State (DOS)

Department of Defense (DOD)

Department of Justice (DOJ)

Department of the Interior (DOI)

Department of Agriculture (USDA)

Department of Labor (DOL)

Department of Health and Human Services (HHS)

Department of Transportation (DOT)

Department of Education (ED)

Department of Homeland Security (DHS)

Domestic Policy Council (DPC)

National Security Staff (NSS)

Office of Management and Budget (OMB)

Office of the Director of National Intelligence (ODNI)

Federal Bureau of Investigation (FBI)

U.S. Agency for International Development (USAID)

U.S. Equal Employment Opportunity Commission (EEOC)

TABLE OF CONTENTS

OVERARCHING THEMES

EXECUTIVE SUMMARY

In commemoration of the 150th anniversary of the Emancipation Proclamation, the Obama Administration reaffirmed the American values of freedom and equality by asking federal agencies to develop a plan to strengthen services for victims of human trafficking. Coordination, Collaboration, Capacity, the *Federal Strategic Action Plan on Services for Victims of Human Trafficking in the United States, 2013-2017* (the Plan) embraces these principles and builds on the progress that our Nation has made in combating human trafficking and modern day forms of slavery through government action, as well as partnerships with allied professionals and concerned citizens.

As our understanding of the scope and impact of human trafficking evolved over the years, we now recognize a more complex web of exploitation affecting diverse communities across the country. Today, we acknowledge that human trafficking affects U.S. citizens and foreign nationals, adults and children, and men, women, and transgender individuals who are victimized across a wide range of commercial sex and forced labor schemes. This Plan details a series of coordinated actions to strengthen the reach and effectiveness of services provided to all victims of human trafficking, regardless of the victims' race, color, national origin, disability, religion, age, gender, immigration status, sexual orientation, or the type of trafficking they endured.

The purpose of this Plan is to describe the steps that federal agencies will take to ensure that all victims of human trafficking in the United States are identified and have access to the services they need to recover. This includes steps to create a victim services network that is comprehensive, trauma-informed, and responsive to the needs of all victims. While prevention and prosecution activities fall outside the scope of this document, the Administration recognizes that addressing human trafficking through prevention, exploring and implementing demand reduction strategies, and using prosecution to hold offenders accountable are critical elements in the U.S. Government's comprehensive approach to combating all forms of human trafficking. The Plan focuses on providing and coordinating support for victims and it aligns with all other efforts of the Federal Government to eliminate human trafficking and prevent further victimization, particularly as outlined in the *Attorney General's Annual Report to Congress and Assessment of U.S. Government Activities to Combat Trafficking in Persons.*[1]

The Plan identifies several "core values" (page 9) related to trafficking victims' services and key areas for improving service delivery. Recognizing that government alone cannot stop this insidious crime, the Plan is written to appeal to a wide audience in order to bring additional resources, expertise, and partnerships to end human trafficking and better support victims. For example, public awareness must be increased to engage more stakeholders and increase victim identification. There must also be an expansion of access to victim services. Finally, the quality of the services, not merely the quantity, must be addressed to ensure that victims are supported throughout their long-term journey as survivors.

The Plan lays out four goals, eight objectives, and contains more than 250 associated action items for victim service improvements that can be achieved during the next 5 years. Federal agencies will coordinate efforts and work toward each of these goals simultaneously. Actions to improve victim identification are woven through each of the goals. The four goals are:

1. ALIGN EFFORTS:
Promote a strategic, coordinated approach to the provision of services for victims of human trafficking at the federal, regional, state, territorial, tribal, and local levels. (page 11)

2. IMPROVE UNDERSTANDING:
Expand and coordinate human trafficking-related research, data, and evaluation to support evidence-based practices in victim services. (page 18)

3. EXPAND ACCESS TO SERVICES:
Provide and promote outreach, training, and technical assistance to increase victim identification and expand the availability of services. (page 24)

4. IMPROVE OUTCOMES:
Promote effective, culturally appropriate, trauma-informed services that improve the short- and long term health, safety, and well-being of victims. (page 38)

While the Plan relies on the framework of the current budget and existing statutory authority, there are several actions included that federal agencies would like to take in the future should funding become available. A timeline for completion of each action and the responsible federal agency is included in Appendix B.

Traditionally, individual federal agencies provide support to victims within their particular areas of responsibility. Coordinating anti-human trafficking efforts at the federal level is crucial to ensuring victims receive comprehensive services. Additionally, federal support will encourage regional, state, territorial, tribal, and local leaders to increase their engagement in and commitment to combating both sex trafficking and labor trafficking and supporting the victims of these crimes. To build community capacity for truly improved victim outreach and services, federal agencies will engage business, philanthropic, and civic leaders, thereby bringing the full expertise and resources of the country to bear in this effort.

The interagency development of the Plan, informed by survivor and stakeholder input and the coordination of current action items, may be the most important aspect of this Plan. A list of the organizations that provided written feedback on the Plan is included in Appendix C. No single federal agency has the expertise, resources, or authorization to address fully the needs of human trafficking victims in the United States; however, by pooling the diverse efforts of the entire Federal Government and working closely with service providers and allied professionals, great progress can be made in the next 5 years.

Continued engagement among federal partners, stakeholders, and communities is needed to truly make the vision of a comprehensive, trauma-informed, and sustainable victim service response a reality. Federal partners, in coordination with the Senior Policy Operating Group, will continue to meet regularly to implement the actions detailed within the Plan and review progress made. Federal partners will also assess the gaps in the Plan and develop collaborative strategies to address identified needs. Federal agencies are committed to maintaining this Plan as a living document, serving as a roadmap for future initiatives.

PLAN DEVELOPMENT

"In the months ahead, we will continue to take action by empowering investigators and law enforcement with the training they need, and by engaging businesses, advocates, and students in developing cutting-edge tools people can use to stay safe."

— President Barack Obama, December 31, 2012

The Plan is a part of the Obama Administration's ongoing efforts to combat human trafficking at home and abroad, and it builds on the strong record of the President's Interagency Task Force to Monitor and Combat Trafficking in Persons. President Obama announced the development of the Plan in his September 25, 2012, remarks to the Clinton Global Initiative, during which he pledged to "do even more to help victims recover and rebuild their lives. We'll develop a new action plan to improve coordination across the Federal Government. We're increasing access to services to help survivors become self-sufficient."

Development of the Plan was a collaborative, multi-phase effort across agencies, led by co-chairs from the Departments of Justice (DOJ), Health and Human Services (HHS) and Homeland Security (DHS).

Phase I: Initial Framework

The co-chairs drafted the framework and key elements of the Plan with input from other members of the Senior Policy Operating Group (SPOG) and other relevant agencies. Federal partners first identified efforts that are currently planned by their departments and component agencies. HHS, along with the other co-chairs, then convened a multidisciplinary stakeholder meeting at the White House on December 10, 2012. Participants included survivors, law enforcement, victim service experts, nonprofit groups, and academia who met to identify gaps in services for human trafficking victims in the United States. That input helped to strengthen the core values and guiding principles on which this Plan is built, provide concrete action steps in the short term, and identify the many issues and steps that must be taken in the short and long term in order to improve victim services and combat human trafficking.

Phase II: Expansion and Publication

On April 9, 2013, the Initial Framework of the Plan was released for a public comment period of 45 days. The purpose of this public comment period was to provide an opportunity for stakeholders, experts within the trafficking field, and the general public to review the Plan, make recommendations to strengthen it, and suggest additional items that can be accomplished through federal collaboration with states, territories, tribes, and local communities or partners to improve the Nation's response to victims of human trafficking.

The Plan was widely disseminated and a Web site established to receive public comments in a transparent forum where stakeholders could read and respond to the comments of others. Additionally, there were six national and regional listening sessions held via conference call and in-person meetings. Stakeholders were invited to submit written comments by mail and e-mail. In this process, 497 distinct comments on the Plan were received via the interactive Web site, and an additional 67 letters and messages were received via e-mail.

The public comments became a central point of discussion during Phase II. The co-chairs facilitated weekly federal interagency meetings over a 2 month period. The purpose of the interagency meetings was to discuss public feedback and to identify areas and strategies for enhanced collaboration. Public comments were shared with SPOG members and other relevant agencies. They were distributed to many program offices and bureaus within each agency to ensure that all could use the comments throughout the development or implementation phases of any human trafficking-related effort. The co-chairs of this strategic planning effort then updated the Plan by incorporating new and revised action items submitted by federal partners.

Published in early 2014, the Plan identifies new strategies to enhance victim services at the federal, regional, state, territorial, tribal, and local levels, and incorporates actionable stakeholder feedback received during the public comment period. While not all of the comments received from the public are reflected in the Plan directly, all were taken into account in the revision of the Plan. The receipt of stakeholder feedback is invaluable to federal efforts, and the comments will be used to inform future program planning.

Phase III: Accountability

Accountability and transparency are critical to ensuring the success of the Plan; thus, the process is driven by realistic goals with concrete action items that clearly outline which departments are responsible for each action and what year completion of each action is anticipated.

This Plan covers a 5-year period; however, in order to fully meet the goals and make the vision of a network of sustainable, comprehensive, and trauma-informed services a reality, the Plan depends on a diverse array of public and private partners working collaboratively with federal agencies to leverage resources effectively over a longer term. The Plan aims to have a lasting impact by developing ideas that can be replicated or scaled and that focus on systemic solutions, innovative ideas, and promising practices.

HHS, DHS, and DOJ, in coordination with the SPOG, will continue to support ongoing federal agency engagement of the goals, objectives, and action items detailed in the Plan. The co-chairs will facilitate quarterly meetings of the SPOG's Victim Services Committee, and coordinate closely with other Committee co-chairs, in order to report on the ongoing implementation of actions. A variety of interagency processes will be used to implement the actions outlined in the Plan and to make those efforts sustainable. Co-chairs and federal partners will continue to engage in dialogue and information gathering to improve the outcomes and impact of action items.

To ensure the ongoing accountability of the Federal Government, and to ensure that the Plan remains adaptive as the anti-human trafficking field continues to grow, the co-chairs, in coordination with all SPOG Committee co-chairs, will collect, compile, and report updates from all federal partners to the President's Interagency Task Force to Monitor and Combat Trafficking in Persons on an annual basis. Annual reporting will include status updates on action items that were due for completion during the previous fiscal year and, where possible, include outcome data for action items. Outcome measurements may include indicators such as the number of individuals within the target audience reached during outreach events, awareness activities, or various in-person and online trainings. Other measurements may include: the number of materials distributed, new tools and resources developed, number of hits on a Web site or training downloads, outreach resources, research reports, and the number of research efforts completed each year. This annual report will be available publicly so that federal agencies remain transparent and communicative on progress made. Each annual report will include the results for the year and, to the extent possible, will show cumulative results on goals and objectives over the duration of the Strategic Action Plan.

Human Trafficking in the United States

An Overview

Human trafficking, also known as trafficking in persons or modern day slavery, is a crime that involves the exploitation of a person for the purpose of compelled labor or a commercial sex act. While the Department of Justice (DOJ) has long enforced criminal laws against involuntary servitude and slavery, the enactment of the Trafficking Victims Protection Act (TVPA)[2] in 2000 was a turning point. The United States directed its efforts to combat human trafficking toward the prosecution of traffickers, the protection of victims, and the prevention of the crime using the TVPA's expanded criminal statutes and newly introduced victim protections and anti-human trafficking programs. This strategy is often referred to as the "3Ps," prevention, protection, and prosecution. A fourth "P," for partnership, is a crucial approach that underlies U.S. anti-trafficking efforts. Since 2000, Congress maintained support for this framework by reauthorizing the TVPA four times, in 2003, 2005, 2008, and 2013.

Under the TVPA, eligibility for victim services[3] is limited to victims of a "severe form of trafficking in persons," which is defined as:

> sex trafficking [i.e., the recruitment, harboring, transportation, provision, or obtaining of a person for the purpose of a commercial sex act] in which a commercial sex act is induced by force, fraud, or coercion, or in which the person induced to perform such act has not attained 18 years of age; or

> the recruitment, harboring, transportation, provision, or obtaining of a person for the purpose of labor or services, through the use of force, fraud, or coercion for the purpose of subjection to involuntary servitude, peonage, debt bondage, or slavery.[4]

While it is difficult to measure the magnitude of human trafficking, the International Labour Organization estimates that more than 20 million men, women, and children are victimized by forced labor and sex trafficking worldwide, including in the United States.[5] Many of these victims are lured with false promises of well-paying jobs or manipulated by people they trust. They are forced or coerced into prostitution, domestic servitude, or other types of forced labor. Victims can be found in legitimate and illegitimate labor industries, including sweatshops, massage parlors, agriculture, restaurants, hotels, and domestic service.

Statutory Framework and Government Response

The TVPA created stronger tools for prosecutors, including increased penalties, mandatory restitution for victims, and funding for victim services. Subsequent reauthorizations further strengthened prosecutorial tools, awareness efforts, and support for victims in response to an enhanced understanding of human trafficking. For instance, the Trafficking Victims Protection Reauthorization Act of 2003[6] mandated new information campaigns, including public-private partnerships to combat sex tourism; required an annual report from the Attorney General to Congress about federal efforts to combat trafficking; and created a new civil cause of action allowing victims of trafficking to sue their traffickers in federal district court. The Trafficking Victims Protection Reauthorization Act of 2005[7] authorized new anti-human trafficking resources, including grant assistance programs to expand victim assistance programs to U.S. citizens or lawful permanent residents who were victims of trafficking. The William Wilberforce Trafficking Victims Protection Reauthorization Act of 2008[8] added measures to increase the effectiveness of anti-human trafficking programs, expand T visa protections, and strengthen the investigation and prosecution of human trafficking, among other things. Finally, the most recent TVPA reauthorization, which was included in the Violence Against Women Reauthorization Act of 2013, enhanced support for state, territorial, tribal, and local efforts to address human trafficking investigations, prosecutions, and victim services, with a particular focus on the sex trafficking of minors.

The President's Interagency Task Force to Monitor and Combat Trafficking in Persons (PITF), a statutorily established, Cabinet-level coordinating task force chaired by the Secretary of State, brings together federal departments and agencies to address all aspects of human trafficking through a whole-of-government approach, including criminal and labor law enforcement, victim identification and protection, education and public awareness, international development, enhanced partnerships and research opportunities, and international engagement and diplomacy. The member and invited agencies of the PITF are the Department of State (DOS), Department of Defense (DOD), Department of Justice (DOJ), Department of the Interior (DOI), Department of Agriculture (USDA), Department of Labor (DOL), Department of Health and Human Services (HHS), Department of Transportation (DOT), Department of Education (ED), Department of Homeland Security (DHS), the Domestic Policy Council (DPC), the National Security Staff (NSS), the Office of Management and Budget (OMB), the Office of the Director of National Intelligence (ODNI), the Federal Bureau of Investigation (FBI), the U.S. Agency for International Development (USAID), and the U.S. Equal Employment Opportunity Commission (EEOC). Senior officials designated as representatives of the PITF principals convene routinely as the Senior Policy Operating Group to carry out the priorities set by the PITF.

State and local governments have increasingly built stronger response systems against human trafficking affecting their communities. Today, all states have enacted laws to better protect victims of human trafficking and enhance prosecution efforts, while continuing to identify ways to adapt to the changing methods used by human traffickers. DOJ's U.S. Attorneys' Offices and federal, state, territorial, tribal, and local law enforcement coordinate with community-based victim service providers in federally funded task forces to strengthen enforcement efforts. Mayors' offices and city councils are increasingly appointing committees to identify gaps in services for victims of human trafficking and are partnering with the private sector and nongovernmental organizations, including faith-based communities, to help trafficking victims recover and rebuild their lives. State and county child protection workers and educators are also increasingly recognizing and responding to human trafficking and how it impacts the lives of youth in their care.

Victims of Human Trafficking

Victims of human trafficking come from all walks of life and are entrapped in many different settings. Victims can be anyone, regardless of race, color, national origin, disability, religion, age, gender, sexual orientation, gender identity, socioeconomic status, or citizenship status. While there is no defining characteristic that all victims share, traffickers frequently prey on individuals who are poor, vulnerable, living in an unsafe situation, or are in search of a better life. These victims are deceived by false promises of love, a good job, or a stable life, and lured into situations where they are forced to work under deplorable conditions with little to no pay. Whether made to work in agriculture, a factory, or a strip club, forced into commercial sex, or abused in a home as a domestic servant, federal law recognizes these people as victims of human trafficking.

The cases tell stories of a single trafficker who works alone to deceive and prey on victims; of families that have been in the business of human trafficking for generations; and of front businesses that appear legitimate at first glance but disguise human trafficking. Prosecutors have successfully demonstrated

that someone can be enslaved without chains and that traffickers often go beyond physical abuse and use extreme forms of psychological abuse that exploit vulnerabilities to maintain control over victims and prevent them from escaping. To achieve their ends, traffickers instill fear of arrest or deportation, use threats of harm to a family member, perpetuate shame or guilt about what is happening, and warn of financial ruin. These experiences are traumatizing and often result in psychological dissociation, distrust, and gaps in the victim's memory that make recounting a clear and complete story difficult. In addition, traffickers sometimes promote drug dependencies among their victims, keeping the victims reliant on the trafficker for access to the substances that fuel addiction.[9] Law enforcement officers, prosecutors, and victim advocates learned that the unique and complex abuses inflicted on these victims demand a comprehensive and sustained trauma-informed approach.

Providing Effective, Comprehensive Services to Victims

Trafficking victims typically require numerous types of emergency and long-term services. Needed services include intensive case management, victim advocacy, shelter/housing, food, medical and dental care, mental health treatment, substance abuse treatment, support groups, interpretation/translation services, immigration and other legal assistance, literacy education, and employment and training services.[10]

Primary sources of federal grant funding for services specific to trafficking victims are the HHS Office of Refugee Resettlement and the DOJ Office for Victims of Crime. When victims are involved in trafficking investigations and prosecutions, some victim assistance is also provided by system-based victim/witness coordinators and victim specialists housed within federal agencies such as DOJ's U.S. Attorneys' Offices and the Federal Bureau of Investigation, and DHS's U.S. Immigration and Customs Enforcement Homeland Security Investigations. Victims of human trafficking are also regularly identified and served by individuals working with related vulnerable populations such as child welfare systems, runaway and homeless youth programs, and domestic violence shelters.[11]

Services offered to victims of human trafficking vary greatly across the United States and depend on a number of factors, including the location of the victim; the type of trafficking; the age, gender, disability, and immigration status of a victim; the type of funding available within the community; and the degree to which services within a community are coordinated. All of these factors demonstrate the complexity of the issue and the challenge of ensuring that all victims of human trafficking have access to comprehensive and specialized services that address their specific needs and aid in their full recovery.[12]

Areas for Improvement

After passing the TVPA, the Federal Government made significant improvements in developing a comprehensive victim-centered approach to fight human trafficking; however, there is more to do to ensure that trafficked persons have the tools to move forward and pursue a path of their own choosing. This Plan, developed with input from survivors and other stakeholders, addresses identified areas for improvement with strategies to enhance existing services and strengthen the ways the United States responds to the needs of human trafficking victims.

Enhance coordination and improve guidance. Stakeholders identified a lack of consistent guidance from the Federal Government as a barrier to coordinated service provision. Differences in how human trafficking is defined and described, including among the various Federal Government agencies dealing with the issue, were also cited as a challenge for service providers who try to navigate the federal system on behalf of victims.[13] They spoke about the confusion in working with agencies that have different or overlapping authorities and the potential benefits of using common best practices and guidance that span multiple federal agencies.[14] They expressed concern at the lengthy and complicated process of connecting victims with available services and the lack of standards for these services.[15]

Stakeholders also identified opportunities for enhanced victim identification through better coordination, information sharing, training, and engagement among federal agencies and state and local enforcement and inspection entities, including engagement of entire communities, philanthropic organizations, businesses, and medical and social service professionals.[16] Finally, they stressed the need to include survivors of human trafficking in developing and evaluating policies and initiatives.[17]

Expand data collection and research efforts. Data collection and evidence-based research are sorely needed to inform federal, state, territorial, tribal, local, and nongovernmental organization service provision.[18] Current statistics on human trafficking are limited. Additionally, vulnerable populations and men and boys are often under-identified as victims, further driving unreliable statistics. The need for formal evaluation of programs was identified by stakeholders so that effective services and evidence-based practices can be identified.[19]

Enhance understanding and awareness. Human trafficking is a hidden crime. There is a lack of understanding of how to identify victims of human trafficking—not just by the public, government officials, and law enforcement, but by victims who may not believe or understand that they are the victims of a crime.[20] It is critical that those who may encounter victims of human trafficking are able to recognize the indicators of the crime. For example, public comments on the Plan noted a need for increased awareness among school personnel and other youth-serving agencies in order to better identify minor victims of human trafficking.[21] Additionally, there is a wide variation among state and local law enforcement and service providers across the United States in understanding the services that are available to victims.[22]

Overcome resource constraints and limitations in access to services. Service providers report that additional resources from both government and nongovernmental sources are needed to provide comprehensive long-term victim care and key legal services for all victims.[23] There are also particularly underserved populations, including youth, male, and transgender victims.[24] Service providers also noted that it is challenging to provide access to specialized services tailored to the needs of victims that adequately meet these needs for the full length of time it may take to stabilize a victim.[25]

Stakeholders identified housing and legal services as areas of particular concern. Sustainable housing is a significant issue in achieving long-term recovery and self-sufficiency for human trafficking survivors. Stakeholders expressed concerns about the lack of safe and appropriate housing options that meet the specific needs of varying types of victims. Additionally, crime victims face an array of legal needs resulting from their victimization, and human trafficking victims are no exception. Because foreign-born victims may not have legal status in the United States, they may be reluctant to come forward. Traffickers also use victims' lack of legal status to exploit and control them. While human trafficking victims may be eligible for T or U nonimmigrant status, which allows victims to remain and work in the United States and assist law enforcement authorities in the investigation or prosecution of human trafficking cases, many victims continue to face legal constraints challenging their recovery process. The integration of the legal services network into the victim services network is a new effort that will require extensive collaboration and coordination.

This Plan seeks to address these issues.

VICTIM AND SURVIVOR

The Plan uses the terms "victim" and "survivor" to refer to individuals who were trafficked. The term "victim" has legal implications within the criminal justice process and generally means an individual who suffered harm as a result of criminal conduct. "Victims" also have particular rights within the criminal justice process.[26] Federal law enforcement agencies often use the term "victim" as part of their official duties. "Survivor" is a term used by many in the services field to recognize the strength it takes to continue on a journey toward healing in the aftermath of a traumatic experience. In the context of this Plan, which promotes improvements in outreach, identification strategies, and services, both terms are intended to honor those who have suffered, or are suffering, the effects of being trafficked.

VISION

We envision that every victim of human trafficking is identified and provided access to the services they need to recover and rebuild their lives through the creation of a responsive, sustainable, comprehensive, and trauma-informed victim services network that leverages public and private partnerships and resources effectively.

GUIDING PRINCIPLES

These principles helped guide the development process and structure of the Plan:

The Plan should be developed collaboratively across agencies of the Federal Government and with a variety of stakeholders at the state, territorial, tribal, and local levels.

The Plan should be realistic, action-oriented, capable of being implemented given current funding constraints, and user friendly.

The Plan should demonstrate a vision and goals over the long term, but include specific tasks for accomplishment in the next 5 years.

The Plan should be designed to help all partners remain accountable to stakeholders for commitments made.

The impact of the Plan should be lasting and scalable.

The Plan should be driven by solutions and innovation, and it should be based on evidence and lessons learned.

CORE VALUES

Federal partners agreed on the following core values that inform the objectives and action steps outlined in the Plan:

Survivors play a key role in elevating understanding and awareness of human trafficking, improving service delivery, and informing policy. Meaningful engagement with survivors in all aspects of program development, implementation, and evaluation is critical in order to develop effective service networks.

Services should be accessible for all trafficking victims, regardless of race, color, national origin, disability, religion, age, gender, sexual orientation, gender identity, immigration status, or type of trafficking (sex or labor).

Victim services should promote safety, healing, justice, and rights for victims, and should empower them to participate in efforts to bring traffickers to justice.

Public awareness and an understanding of human trafficking at federal, state, territorial, tribal, and local levels are needed to improve victim identification and access to services.

Anti-human trafficking efforts should be victim-centered and culturally relevant, holistic, comprehensive, evidence-based, gender-responsive, and trauma-informed.

All those who engage with survivors must acknowledge and respect an individual's experience of victimization and capacity to move beyond victimization.

Services for long-term needs, in addition to services that address immediate and emergency needs, are critical. Survivors should be provided with tools and opportunities for financial stability that will support their long-term independence.

VICTIM-CENTERED AND TRAUMA-INFORMED APPROACHES

The victim centered approach seeks to minimize retraumatization associated with the criminal justice process by providing the support of victim advocates and service providers, empowering survivors as engaged participants in the process, and providing survivors an opportunity to play a role in seeing their traffickers brought to justice. In this manner, the victim centered approach plays a critical role in supporting a victim's rights, dignity, autonomy, and self determination, while simultaneously advancing the government's and society's interest in prosecuting traffickers to condemn and deter this reprehensible crime. An understanding of a victim centered approach in the United States developed over time to respond to the needs of crime victims and continues to evolve as we learn new lessons and establish promising practices.

A trauma informed approach includes an understanding of the physical, social, and emotional impact of trauma on the individual, as well as on the professionals who help them. A trauma informed approach includes victim centered practices, as it is implemented with trauma impacted populations. A program, organization, or system that is trauma informed realizes the widespread impact of trauma and understands potential paths for healing; recognizes the signs and symptoms of trauma in staff, clients, and others involved with the system; and responds by fully integrating knowledge about trauma into policies, procedures, practices, and settings.[27] Like a victim centered approach, the priority is on the victim's safety and security and on safeguarding against policies and practices that may inadvertently retraumatize victims.

GOAL 1: ALIGN EFFORTS

Promote a strategic, coordinated approach to the provision of services for victims of human trafficking at the federal, regional, state, territorial, tribal, and local levels.

In order to leverage resources, maximize effectiveness, and reduce burdens on direct service providers, it is critical to coordinate federal response efforts. Federal efforts should be coordinated and complementary, not contradictory and confusing. Federal agencies recognize that while building capacity and improving the response to victims within their own agency is a critical step, it is not enough. Increased coordination and collaboration among federal agencies, and between public and private partners, is needed to further develop and sustain a comprehensive and trauma-informed service network for victims of human trafficking.

The creation of this Plan is one of many actions the Obama Administration is taking to coordinate the Federal Government's approach to combat human trafficking and assist victims. Prioritization of human trafficking among federal leadership, with an emphasis on the need for strategic collaboration, sends an important message about the urgency of these efforts and sheds light on this hidden crime.

To reach this goal, federal actions fall under two objectives:

OBJECTIVE 1: Provide federal leadership and direction to improve victim services.

OBJECTIVE 2: Coordinate victim services effectively through collaboration across multiple service sectors.

RESPONSIBLE ENTITIES

The Plan describes some action items at the Department level (e.g., HHS) when more than one component within the Department will carry out the action, or when it is a Department wide initiative. Most action items detail the Department's component level (e.g., HHS's Administration for Children and Families) to identify the specific offices within each Department that are responsible for each action item. For clarification of Department and component names, refer to page 45 for a complete list of acronyms used in the Plan.

INTEGRATE SURVIVOR EXPERIENCES AND INPUT

Responses to victimization must retain a focus on the needs, beliefs, and interests of the victims. The Federal Government recognizes that engaging survivors in anti human trafficking leadership and decisionmaking is imperative to providing effective services. This is a core value of the Plan, implicitly woven through each goal and often discussed in federal interagency meetings.

Feedback received during the public comment period reinforced the importance of this effort. Survivors expressed a desire to do more than share their stories to educate the public about human trafficking; they want to be included in the development of programs, policies, strategies, and materials.

Federal agencies, including HHS, DHS, DOJ, DOS's Office to Monitor and Combat Trafficking in Persons, and the EEOC, will work in coordination with the Senior Policy Operating Group to develop a collaborative approach to explore partnerships with survivor groups in order to seek ongoing input from survivors on initiatives and policies. Specific agency efforts include:

➤ DOJ's Office for Victims of Crime, in coordination with DHS, DOS's Office to Monitor and Combat Trafficking in Persons, HHS's Administration for Children and Families, and other DOJ component offices, including the Executive Office for United States Attorneys and the Community Oriented Policing Services Office, will host a survivor forum to hear from survivors on effective, strategic, and meaningful ways to engage survivor groups and incorporate their perspectives.

➤ DHS will continue to engage nongovernmental stakeholders, including survivors, in meetings twice a year. These meetings will update stakeholders on recent activities and provide a platform for participants to offer individual feedback regarding current DHS Blue Campaign efforts.

➤ HHS's Administration for Children and Families, DHS's U. S. Immigration and Customs Enforcement Homeland Security Investigations Victim Assistance Program, and DOJ's FBI and Office for Victims of Crime will integrate survivor experiences and perspectives into training and technical assistance materials designed for victim assistance specialists, law enforcement agencies, and service providers.

➤ DOJ's Executive Office for United States Attorneys will distribute guidance to the U.S. Attorneys' Offices' human trafficking task forces encouraging them to seek survivor input where appropriate.

➤ HHS's Administration for Children and Families will explore the creation of a public platform to receive ongoing feedback on the quality of services accessed by survivors of human trafficking, including gaps in services and challenges to service delivery.

OBJECTIVE 1:

Provide federal leadership and direction to improve victim services.

Federal agencies will take a leadership role to improve the alignment and effectiveness of victim services systems through the implementation of recommendations for systematic change and identification of promising practices. This Plan will provide the roadmap for federal efforts to develop innovative strategies to advance the anti-human trafficking field. In addition, the Federal Government will explore ways to promote this Plan and encourage states and localities to inform and align efforts to multiply their impact. The Federal Government recognizes the major contributions and critical role that states and localities play in victim services, and is ready to ensure federal efforts coordinate and enhance this work.

Implement Recommendations For Systematic Change

There are myriad government systems and programs, including refugee resettlement agencies, public health agencies, and crime victim compensation, that identify, serve, and support human trafficking victims. Fragmentation and lack of awareness in these systems are identified as barriers to victim identification and effective victim services.

The Federal Government will solicit, publish, and implement field-driven recommendations to align and improve victim services across various systems. These efforts will improve access to services for victims, ensure that government services are more responsive to the needs of human trafficking victims, provide the field with further guidance and direction, and assist in the identification and promotion of promising practices.

➤ DOJ's Office of Juvenile Justice and Delinquency Prevention will work to implement the recommendations of the 2012 report of the Attorney General's National Task Force on Children Exposed to Violence, _Defending Childhood: Protect, Heal, Thrive_ (www.justice.gov/ defendingchildhood/cev-rpt-full.pdf). A subcommittee

of the Coordinating Council on Juvenile Justice and Delinquency Prevention will be formed to address agency responsibilities and a timeline for implementing recommendations. Partners include HHS's Administration for Children and Families, Substance Abuse and Mental Health Services Administration, and Centers for Disease Control and Prevention; DOI; Corporation for National and Community Service; USDA; and DOJ's Office for Victims of Crime and Office on Violence Against Women.

➤ The Task Force on American Indian/Alaska Native (AI/ AN) Children Exposed to Violence, created in response to recommendations of the Attorney General's National Task Force on Children Exposed to Violence, will conduct public hearings and listening sessions in AI/ AN communities to help the AI/AN Task Force gain a fuller understanding of the issues surrounding AI/AN children's exposure to violence, including the impact of human trafficking on AI/AN children.

➤ DOJ's Office for Victims of Crime will publish _Vision 21: Transforming Victim Services_, which includes extensive recommendations on improving strategic planning, research, capacity building, and funding for services, including specific references to human trafficking victims and the provision of comprehensive legal services, including steps that could be taken if additional funding could be brought to bear. The Office for Victims of Crime will expand legal assistance capacity for victims of human trafficking through current policy, programming, and funding.

➤ DHS, DOS's Office to Monitor and Combat Trafficking in Persons, HHS, and USAID will review and work with faith-based and other community-based organizations and leaders, as appropriate, to implement recommendations to combat human trafficking as outlined in the 2013 report of the President's Advisory Council on Faith-based and Neighborhood Partnerships, _Building Partnerships to Eradicate Modern Day Slavery (http:// www.whitehouse.gov/sites/default/files/docs/advisory_ council_humantrafficking_report.pdf)._

➤ HHS's Administration for Children and Families will rollout guidance on child trafficking for the child welfare and

"Coordination among federal agencies on funding is vital to expanding anti-human trafficking efforts. Lack of funding is often cited as a challenge to trafficking investigations and services, which go hand in hand. Creative or additional means of funding should be sought. Solicitations for joint grants should be concise and reviewed carefully for contradictory requirements."

– Indiana Office of the Attorney General

runaway and homeless youth systems on understanding trends in victimization, runaway patterns, and assessment and service delivery upon the return of such individuals. The guidance builds on best existing practices in victim services in related fields, such as domestic and sexual violence victim service programs.

Identify Promising Practices

While victim services were developed over the course of more than a decade, the anti-human trafficking field only recently matured to a place where promising practices can be identified. New service providers and veteran organizations expanding their missions to meet the needs of this emerging population are seeking reliable information on the effectiveness of the various approaches employed in the field.

Federal agencies will identify emerging and promising practices that show evidence of effectiveness as an immediate first step. Long-term impact studies are needed to reinforce these designations. These resources will begin to form a practice base, available to federal agencies and nongovernmental organizations, from which evidence-based practices can be developed. In addition, the Federal Government will explore ways to promote this Plan and encourage states and localities to inform and align efforts to multiply their impact.

➤ Federal agencies, including DHS, DOJ, DOS's Office to Monitor and Combat Trafficking in Persons, ED, and HHS, will explore convening meetings where allied professionals share lessons learned with federal agencies to inform the development of federal anti-human trafficking efforts.

➤ DOJ's Office on Violence Against Women, in consultation with HHS's Administration for Children and Families, will gather input from expert stakeholders on the role domestic violence and sexual assault victim service providers play in addressing human trafficking and identifying promising practices related to sex trafficking of minors.

➤ DOJ's National Institute of Justice will release a Research Triangle Institute evaluation of the Fiscal Year 2009 DOJ *Office for Victims of Crime Services to Domestic Minor*

STANDARDS OF CARE

Many providers are developing new programs and services to meet the needs of human trafficking victims in their communities. Stakeholders clearly expressed interest in the promulgation of uniform standards of care to shape and make consistent the quality of care provided for victims of human trafficking. Comprehensive standards of care will guide the development of programs that are effective, trauma informed, culturally appropriate, gender appropriate, and protect the safety of staff and clients alike. Federal agencies recognize the value of standards of care and are committed to working collaboratively toward this goal. Initial steps to move this initiative forward include:

➤ DOJ's Office for Victims of Crime will publish Achieving Excellence: Model Standards for Serving Victims & Survivors of Crime. These Model Standards were developed by a broad based consortium of victim service experts at the federal, state, territorial, tribal, and local levels, including providers experienced in serving victims of human trafficking, domestic violence, sexual assault, and other crimes. The publication will include updated program, competency, and ethical standards, and will promote the competence and ethical integrity of providers and quality and consistency of program services in all settings serving crime victims.

➤ HHS's Administration for Children and Families, in coordination with DHS and DOJ, will identify minimum standards of care required by grant recipients providing services to victims of human trafficking.

Victims of Human Trafficking grants, which identifies promising practices in developing programs for trafficked youth.

➤ DOJ's Office for Victims of Crime, in consultation with federal partners, will publish a survivor-created guide on developing culturally competent services for commercially sexually exploited and trafficked girls and young women.

➤ HHS's Administration for Children and Families will assess and disseminate analysis of the impact, strengths, and challenges of any pilot program on human trafficking within the runaway and homeless youth program.

➤ HHS's Administration for Children and Families and Substance Abuse and Mental Health Services Administration will provide a series of recommendations on meeting the mental health needs of victims. This follows up on the Assistant Secretary for Planning and Evaluation's 2008 National Symposium on the Health Needs of Human Trafficking Victims.

OBJECTIVE 2:

Coordinate victim services effectively through collaboration across multiple service sectors.

Federal government agencies are in a unique position to work across multiple sectors. Stakeholders expressed a strong interest in federal efforts to better align the work of all agencies.[28] Federal agencies will participate in ongoing meetings, in coordination with the Senior Policy Operating Group, to ensure that various federal anti-human trafficking efforts are strategic and complementary. Increased collaboration and coordination within the Federal Government and among all levels of government will leverage resources, reduce duplication of efforts, and help to create a strong and consistent victim service network across the United States.

Develop and Promote Standard Terminology

Differences in how human trafficking is defined and described, including among the various Federal Government agencies dealing with the issue, are cited as a challenge for service providers and regional, state, territorial, tribal, and local government agencies that try to navigate the federal service system on behalf of victims.[29] Feedback received during the 45-day public comment period for the Plan stressed the importance of this effort and the need to align definitions at the onset of the 5-year Plan to ensure that any training and technical assistance materials developed under the plan use clear and consistent messaging.

Federal agencies, in coordination with the Senior Policy Operating Group, will engage in ongoing conversations to provide coordinated leadership and direction around terminology. Agencies will discuss differences in terminology, identify common terms, and provide recommendations to reduce confusion and enhance coordination.

➤ DOJ's Office for Victims of Crime will collaborate with DHS, DOL, DOS's Office to Monitor and Combat Trafficking in Persons, EEOC, HHS's Administration for Children and Families, and other DOJ components, including the Office of Community Oriented Policing Services, to update, translate, print, and disseminate *Trafficking in Persons: A Guide for Non-Governmental Organizations* (previously published in 2002). The publication will set forth common terminology for use by federal agencies in their anti-human trafficking work and can also be used for the purpose of public awareness and education on human trafficking. Federal agencies will seek and incorporate feedback, where appropriate, from survivors, victim service providers, anti-human trafficking organizations, and other stakeholders before updating the publication to ensure that the document reflects perspectives from the field.

➤ HHS's Administration for Children and Families will work with federal partners to clarify the definitions of child sex trafficking and commercial sexual exploitation of children and provide guidance to grantees and service providers. Additionally, the Administration for Children and Families will consider the federal Child Abuse and Prevention and Treatment Act's child maltreatment and caregiver definitions and their impact on services to victims of human trafficking.

➤ DOJ's Office of Community Oriented Policing Services will work to update any publications related to human trafficking to include consistent language, federal statutes, resources, and other pertinent information as provided from federal partners.

Ensure Federal Funding is Strategically Coordinated

Federal funding for direct services, research, and law enforcement efforts are administered by separate agencies throughout the Federal Government. Grant recipients cited challenges when working with multiple federal grants due to discrepancies and gaps in allowable service provision.[30] A strategic, coordinated approach is needed to ensure that all resources are being equitably and effectively distributed.

Federal agencies, in coordination with the Senior Policy Operating Group, will improve their efforts across departments to increase coordination of federal funding. Federal agencies will work to identify anti-human trafficking-specific funding, as well as other federal system funding for vulnerable populations, and provide guidance on how to leverage these resources to better serve the comprehensive needs of diverse trafficking victims.

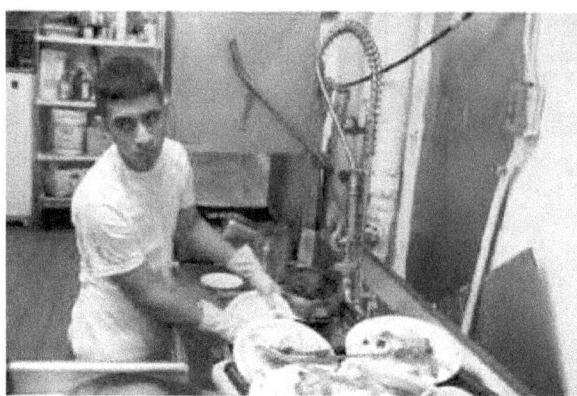
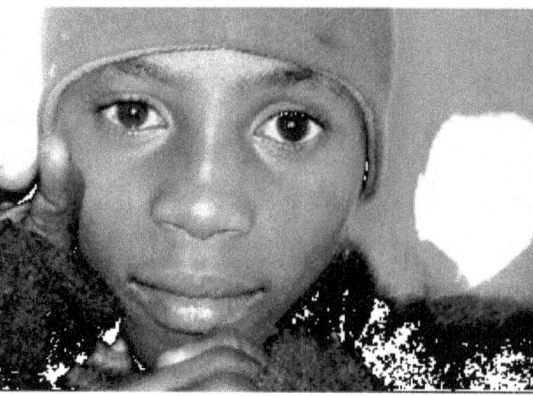

➤ HHS's Administration for Children and Families will explore the costs and possibilities of effective funding models for victim services.

➤ DOJ's Office for Victims of Crime and Office on Violence Against Women, and HHS's Administration for Children and Families will work together to review guidance and solicitation language to coordinate federal funding and to identify opportunities for expanding partnerships, including enhancing the provision of services to victims of human trafficking who are identified via domestic violence shelters, non-residential domestic violence programs, and runaway and homeless youth programs.

➤ DOJ's Office for Victims of Crime and Bureau of Justice Assistance, and HHS's Administration for Children and Families, will consider ways to complement and coordinate grant performance measurements and data collection methods.

➤ DOJ's Office for Victims of Crime and Bureau of Justice Assistance will continue to publish solicitations and award grants for Anti-Human Trafficking Task Forces, which emphasize a multidisciplinary, collaborative effort of law enforcement officials and victim service providers to offer the broadest range of services and resources for victims and the most diverse range of investigation and prosecution options in response to perpetrators.

➤ DOJ's Office on Violence Against Women (OVW) will include human trafficking in grant solicitations where it is allowable and appropriate under the reauthorized Violence Against Women Act (VAWA) statute. OVW will consider prioritizing victims of human trafficking in certain grant solicitations, such as those focused on youth, sexual assault, culturally specific communities, and violence in the workplace. Finally, OVW will incorporate input provided by expert stakeholders, DOJ's Office of Juvenile Justice and Delinquency Prevention and Office for Victims of Crime, and HHS's Administration for Children and Families to enhance service provision and accessibility for victims of human trafficking via existing VAWA grants.

➤ DOJ's Office on Violence Against Women (OVW) will provide guidance to grantees regarding provision of Violence Against Women Act (VAWA) grant-funded services to victims of human trafficking. OVW will also train program managers and other OVW staff on human trafficking issues and how to incorporate human trafficking into VAWA grants. OVW, in conjunction with DOJ's Office of Legislative Affairs, will explore definitions of victims included in VAWA and their impact on services for human trafficking victims.

➤ DOJ's Office of Community Oriented Policing Services, in coordination with other federal agencies, will consider incorporating one topic area or project devoted to human trafficking training in the Fiscal Year 2014 solicitation for Community Policing Development.

➤ DOJ's Office of Juvenile Justice and Delinquency Prevention will continue to engage in ongoing fiscal year program planning that considers support of human trafficking efforts across funding authorities.

Improve Coordination at the National, Regional, State, Territorial, Tribal, and Local Levels

Alignment at the federal level is a critical first step, but the Federal Government must also work effectively with government and nongovernmental organizations at the national, regional, state, territorial, tribal, and local levels to better identify victims and create a seamless victim service network.

Federal agencies, in coordination with the Senior Policy Operating Group, will work to identify and share partnerships with national membership organizations that will foster communication and coordination among national, regional, state, territorial, tribal, and local levels. Federal agencies will collaborate to better support partners, strengthen the efforts of regional and local federal agency offices, and explore ways to encourage states, tribes, and localities to inform and align efforts to multiply their impact.

- Relevant federal agencies will identify regional and local offices and points of contact to assist with communication and collaboration efforts at the regional, state, territorial, tribal, and local levels; receive advanced training, and serve as resources for their agencies in dealing with relevant human trafficking activities.

- DHS, DOJ, and HHS, in coordination with the Senior Policy Operating Group, will convene regular meetings over the next 5 years to coordinate implementation of activities detailed in this Plan, identify opportunities for enhanced coordination, and share reports of Plan implementation activities with the President's Interagency Task Force to Monitor and Combat Trafficking in Persons and the public.

- An internal DOJ Anti-Human Trafficking Working Group will continue to meet quarterly to discuss and coordinate activities across and amongst component agencies. Increased federal task force coordination will be a central part of the ongoing discussions. Additionally, collaborative efforts will be made to link this working group with other DOJ efforts, such as the Access to Justice Initiative and DOJ's Office of Juvenile Justice and Delinquency Prevention's Federal Agency Task Force on Missing and Exploited Children.

- An internal HHS Human Trafficking Working Group will continue to meet at least quarterly to discuss and coordinate activities across and amongst component agencies, including coordination with regional, state, territorial, tribal, and local activities.

- HHS's Administration for Children and Families will explore the possibility of coordinating with the AmeriCorps VISTA program to increase capacity of state and local partners to respond to human trafficking through enhanced volunteer support.

- HHS's Administration for Children and Families will draft a 3-year plan to distribute ideas for innovative outreach programming to grantees and the public through the National Human Trafficking Resource Center, and other channels, in coordination with the Runaway and Homeless Youth Training and Technical Assistance Center, the Child Welfare Information Gateway, the National Resource Center on Domestic Violence, the Asian & Pacific Islander Institute on Domestic Violence, and appropriate HHS Health Resource and Service Administration Bureaus and Offices.

- DHS's Blue Campaign Steering Committee will continue to meet regularly and will be accountable to define and prioritize crosscutting strategic projects for all human trafficking-related capabilities for DHS. Additionally, the Blue Campaign Steering Committee will identify areas where Departmental resources can be leveraged more effectively, recommend program enhancements, and share best practices and lessons learned across the Department.

- DOS will continue to address the protection of A-3 and G-5 workers through its regular internal working group meeting on domestic worker issues, where it reviews allegations and cases and discusses strategies and ongoing efforts to prevent abuse and obtain compliance with DOS requirements. DOS will continue to streamline referrals of potential victims to the Department's Bureau of Diplomatic Security, which coordinates with DOJ and other agencies, as appropriate, to investigate allegations of abuse and available services.

- DOS will continue to brief stakeholders annually, including nongovernmental organizations, to raise awareness about efforts to protect and identify victims of trafficking.

GOAL 2: IMPROVE UNDERSTANDING

Expand and coordinate human trafficking-related research, data, and evaluation to support evidence-based practices in victim services.

Due to the hidden and complex nature of the crime, the full scope of human trafficking in the United States is unknown. Statistics related to vulnerable populations and men and boys may be particularly unreliable. While rough estimates are available, increased efforts and improved means for research, data collection, and evaluation would improve the understanding of the prevalence of the crime, the needs of victims, and the effectiveness of services provided to victims of human trafficking.

The anti-human trafficking field has provided services to victims of human trafficking through various strategies and delivery methods for more than a decade, making great strides in assisting victims to make improvements in their lives. There is an opportunity to conduct research on this effort to identify evidence-based practices in federal, state, territorial, tribal, local, and nongovernmental organization service provision. It is now time to reflect on lessons learned and to begin the process of moving from the use of promising practices to developing evidence-based approaches.

To reach this goal, federal actions fall under two objectives:

OBJECTIVE 3: Establish baseline knowledge of human trafficking and victim service needs through rigorous research and reporting.

OBJECTIVE 4: Support the development of effective responses to the needs of human trafficking victims.

OBJECTIVE 3:

Establish baseline knowledge of human trafficking and victim service needs through rigorous research and reporting.

Federal agencies will continue to work in coordination with the Senior Policy Operating Group to invest in strategic research requirements, such as the prevalence of human trafficking in the United States and the needs of victims. Agencies will identify, collect, evaluate, and share data related to ongoing efforts that will provide more reliable, timely information about human trafficking and the government's response.

Research Human Trafficking in The United States

Research on the effectiveness of service delivery strategies requires the establishment of baseline data and rigorous study of those approaches and outcomes. Reliable information is needed to better understand the prevalence and characteristics of human trafficking in the United States, including both sex and labor trafficking. Additionally, victim service practices should be evaluated so that effective approaches can be scaled and expanded.

Federal agencies, in coordination with the Senior Policy Operating Group, will collaboratively design and implement research priorities to address knowledge gaps. Efforts will be strategically aligned to leverage the work across all federal agencies.

➤ The Senior Policy Operating Group Research and Data Committee will further develop and use a research matrix, cataloguing all U.S. Government-funded research on human trafficking since Fiscal Year 2002, to share information on research projects with the public and to guide Committee discussions about research gaps and future research.

➤ DOJ's National Institute of Justice (NIJ) will release

multiple research and evaluation studies of human trafficking germane to this objective.

- NIJ will release two studies of labor trafficking. One is a Research Triangle Institute study that focuses on developing measures and indicators of labor trafficking in North Carolina, and the other is an Urban Institute study on the nature and characteristics of labor trafficking victimization in the United States.

- The Urban Institute will complete a study that measures the size of the unlawful commercial sex economy in selected communities in the United States.

- NIJ will release a Georgetown University study of the effectiveness of interventions to stabilize, rehabilitate, and integrate foreign national victims into the wider society.

- NIJ will release a Colorado College study that assesses the elements of state-level legislation that are most effective at improving successful prosecutions of trafficking.

- The Research Triangle Institute will conclude a study of the underreporting of trafficked minors in Illinois.

➤ HHS's Administration for Children and Families will examine the results of a 2-year pilot program that is providing foreign national human trafficking victims with pre-employment services prior to certification in order to inform future policy or program changes.

➤ The Fund for the City of New York will complete a DOJ Office of Juvenile Justice and Delinquency Prevention-funded study on the prevalence of the commercial sexual exploitation of children (CSEC), including sex trafficking, in the United States. This study will estimate the size and scope of CSEC in the United States, describe the characteristics and needs of CSEC victims, explore available services, and analyze prosecution outcomes for victims and exploiters.

➤ The National Academy of Sciences will release a DOJ Office of Juvenile Justice and Delinquency Prevention-

"Include quality and impact in the evaluation of responses to human trafficking survivors. So often the focus is on the number of victims identified and how many people become certified or employed. Qualitative research is necessary to adequately assess other important measures of success (e.g., survivors' improved feelings of safety and well being; preparedness to enter the job market; increased engagement in one's community)."

– Northern Tier Anti-Trafficking Consortium

funded study of commercial sexual exploitation of children (CSEC) in the United States, which includes sex trafficking. This study investigates the scope and severity, causes and consequences, intersection with child welfare and juvenile justice systems, evidence-based responses, and international and local policy approaches to CSEC. The study will recommend strategies to respond to CSEC, including sex trafficking, in the United States.

➤ Through a DOJ Office of Juvenile Justice and Delinquency Prevention-funded study, the Urban Institute will assess the characteristics and needs of both the lesbian, gay, bisexual, transgender, and questioning population, and the young men who have sex with men population, who are involved in the commercial sex market to learn about their interactions with law enforcement, prosecutors, and court personnel. In addition, the study will assess how lesbian, gay, bisexual, transgender, and questioning youth enter the criminal justice system, what services are available after detention, and what percentage of youth return to the streets after serving their sentence.

➤ DOJ's Office on Violence Against Women, in partnership with DOJ's National Institute of Justice, will fund a study of the impact of the population boom from an influx of oil workers, in western North Dakota and eastern Montana, on domestic violence, dating violence, sexual assault, stalking, and human trafficking.

Identify Resource Gaps

➤ In order to better target future efforts, an improved understanding of the services currently being provided is needed. The needs of vulnerable and underserved populations are not fully understood, which restricts the ability of providers to appropriately respond to the needs of these victims.

➤ Federal agencies will work in coordination with the Senior Policy Operating Group to strategically collect and share information about gaps on an ongoing basis. This comprehensive effort will leverage the specialized knowledge of each partner in the creation of a more complete understanding of the needs of the entire field.

➤ DOJ's Office for Victims of Crime will collaborate

with DOJ's Bureau of Justice Assistance and the Human Smuggling and Trafficking Center to provide federal agencies with GIS mapping of services, formal collaborations (such as locations of the Office for Victims of Crime/Bureau of Justice Assistance Anti-Human Trafficking Task Forces, Anti-Trafficking Coordination Teams, HHS Rescue and Restore Coalitions, specialized legal services, DOJ Office on Violence Against Women grantees, Internet Crimes Against Children Task Forces, Innocence Lost Task Forces, and Project Safe Childhood Task Forces), and, to the extent the data are available, federal, state, territorial, tribal, and local law enforcement data on locations of human trafficking arrests and investigations. Where appropriate, opportunities to engage technology companies and nonprofit agencies that can add to this effort will be sought. This initiative will assist in identifying gaps in resources and locations that require specific efforts to coordinate and align anti-trafficking initiatives and the provision of victim services.

➤ DOJ's Office of Juvenile Justice and Delinquency Prevention and Office for Victims of Crime will conduct informal assessments of their grant-funded task forces to identify training and technical assistance needs and promising practices.

➤ Federal agencies will collaborate to gather information on under-resourced communities and emerging human trafficking trends and develop strategies to improve services and support.

- DOJ's Office for Victims of Crime and Office on Violence Against Women, and HHS's Administration for Children and Families will gather information from experts and stakeholders on the needs of trafficked American Indian/Alaska Native women and girls and promising practices in service delivery.

- DOJ's Office for Victims of Crime and Office on Violence Against Women and HHS's Administration for Children and Families will gather information from survivors, anti-human trafficking organizations, and service providers on the needs of trafficked boys and men, lesbian, gay, bisexual, transgender, and questioning victims, and minor victims of labor trafficking.

- DOJ's Office on Violence Against Women will explore providing funds to law enforcement and victim service providers in the Bakken area. The Office on Violence Against Women will also host interagency conversations with experts and stakeholders to share information and support these under-resourced rural communities, following up on a site visit to western North Dakota in July 2013, during which local law enforcement, tribal leaders, domestic violence and sexual assault advocates, the U.S. Attorney for North Dakota, state and tribal coalition leaders, and service providers from both western North Dakota and eastern Montana reported increased rates of human trafficking and sexual assault arising from the sudden population boom in the region.

A NOTE ON DATA COLLECTION

It is important to note that data sets from different agencies are collected for different purposes, including program evaluation, grant performance measures, administrative studies, and research studies. These data sets have different parameters and are unlikely to match. When analyzing human trafficking data in the United States, one must take the purpose and context of the data collection into consideration so that the limitations of the data are understood and the statistics are an accurate reflection of U.S. anti human trafficking efforts. Notably, data collection efforts must keep confidentiality and privacy protection of victims in the forefront to ensure that victims remain protected.

Establish New Data Collection Mechanisms

Stakeholders resoundingly agree that a strong baseline understanding of the prevalence of human trafficking in the United States, and the needs of those victims, is needed.[31] The foundation for this baseline lies in the collection, coordination, and sharing of data in a consistent way using common definitions of human trafficking and related terms. Improved and expanded data collection will assist in creating standardized data and help to describe the extent and distribution of human trafficking throughout the United States.

Federal agencies will continue to collaborate on identifying appropriate improvements in data collection efforts. When new data collection efforts are implemented, federal agencies will be clear about the purpose of the data collection.

- ➤ The FBI will build a data collection application to collect end-of-case reporting data for all civil rights investigations, including human trafficking cases. This data will be used for Uniform Crime Reporting purposes, as well as for varied statistical analyses.

- ➤ DOJ's Office of Juvenile Justice and Delinquency Prevention will assist the Internet Crimes Against Children Task Forces, a national network of 61 coordinated task forces representing more than 3,000 federal, state, tribal, and local law enforcement and prosecutorial agencies, to report data on the number of cases related to commercial sexual exploitation of children, including sex trafficking, handled by the Task Forces.

- ➤ DOJ's Office on Violence Against Women will include human trafficking, where appropriate, in grantee and subgrantee report forms. After 2 years of data collection, data will be disseminated by inclusion in reports to Congress.

- ➤ In conjunction with the rule revisions for the Victims of Crime Act Assistance and Compensation Programs, DOJ's Office for Victims of Crime will revise draft grantee and subgrantee data collection forms, which include human trafficking, where appropriate. The Office for Victims of Crime will work in coordination with DOJ's Office on Violence Against Women to align grantee guidance on new data collection instruments as closely as possible.

- ➤ DOJ's National Institute of Justice will host an expert working group, pending approvals, to tackle the methodological barriers hampering data collection and related research efforts on human trafficking.

- ➤ The Human Smuggling and Trafficking Center will convene an interagency working group to explore the value and feasibility of sustaining the data-gathering and analysis that informed the first National Human Trafficking Assessment, including the possibility of more indepth research on particular areas of special interest.

- ➤ EEOC will continue to explore ways of tracking data on human trafficking in its internal data collection systems. EEOC is exploring ways to improve the collection of human trafficking data for charges of discrimination, as well as internal and external outreach events and trainings.

- ➤ HHS's Administration for Children and Families will explore ways, within its existing authorities and using available resources, to better collect data from federal and state data systems and national surveys to support analyses that will uncover specific risk factors for human trafficking among runaway and homeless youth and children who experienced abuse or neglect.

- ➤ HHS's Administration for Children and Families will explore possibilities for improving coordination of data collection on human trafficking across its programs, including refugee resettlement, child welfare, runaway and homeless youth, and domestic violence grantees, where applicable.

- ➤ HHS will explore new data collection strategies, such as 1-day census counts and collecting data through public health methodologies, for compiling unduplicated estimates on the prevalence of human trafficking in the United States.

"Data collection on human trafficking needs improvement. Federal statistics on human trafficking are only capturing a small picture of the problem. Until we have learned to identify all victims of human trafficking, statistics will not be reflective of the full spectrum of victims, including victims who are transgender, female, and male; citizens and foreign nationals; adult and child; sex- and labor-trafficked; free and still in bondage."

– Freedom Network

➤ HHS's Health Resources and Services Administration and intra-agency partners will consider adopting action from the HHS Action Plan to Reduce Racial and Ethnic Health Disparities to establish data standards for information collected related to victims of human trafficking.

Share Data and Reports

Studies of human trafficking have been limited in number and scope. As new and ongoing studies are completed, findings must be shared widely and effectively, both within the Federal Government and with nongovernmental stakeholders, to improve understanding of the dynamics of human trafficking and the effectiveness of current efforts.

In coordination with the Senior Policy Operating Group, federal agencies will collaborate to identify priorities and resources for future research efforts. Additionally, coordinated efforts will be made to better share research conclusions with the field to spur innovations in service provision.

➤ The Human Smuggling and Trafficking Center will share a National Human Trafficking Assessment with relevant federal agencies. This first-ever, interagency human trafficking assessment is based on collated data from more than a dozen federal agencies. It will help the Federal Government allocate law enforcement and other resources by identifying existing and emerging hotspots for trafficking activity across the United States and revealing trends and patterns in victim recruitment and exploitation.

➤ Additionally, the Human Smuggling and Trafficking Center will provide federal agencies a written report of best practices for data collection, data management, and data sharing based on its experience analyzing human trafficking data from more than a dozen federal entities for the National Human Trafficking Assessment. The best practices report will address data collection, storage, standardization, and formatting, as well as policy and privacy considerations relative to data sharing.

➤ The Human Smuggling and Trafficking Center will make the data sets developed for the National Human Trafficking Assessment available to the original data owners. The data sets will contain structured and cleansed data, which the data owner can use for further data reporting or analysis.

➤ DOJ's Office for Victims of Crime will create an annual aggregate data report for public dissemination that includes an indepth analysis of the Office for Victims of Crime's anti-human trafficking grantee performance measurement data.

➤ DOL will collect and make available to federal partners relevant publicly available labor enforcement data aggregated by industry, type, and geographic area regarding labor exploitation.

➤ DHS's U.S. Citizenship and Immigration Services and U.S. Immigration and Customs Enforcement Homeland Security Investigations Victim Assistance Program will work to consolidate existing data on victims of human trafficking and immigration benefits provided to eligible foreign-born victims, including Continued Presence and T and U nonimmigrant visas, and publish the data on the DHS Blue Campaign Web site.

➤ HHS's Administration for Children and Families will release a report analyzing data received from its anti-human trafficking grantees during the first 10 years of victim outreach and service programs.

➤ HHS's Administration for Children and Families will identify the most effective mechanisms to communicate and disseminate analysis of trends on human trafficking through its various training and technical assistance centers.

OBJECTIVE 4:

Support the development of effective responses to the needs of human trafficking victims.

Federal agencies will evaluate and support field-driven initiatives to improve victim identification and services, with the long-term goal of establishing evidenced-based practices. To establish evidence-based practices, federal agencies will continue to identify emerging issues in the human trafficking field and engage stakeholders in defining and describing the challenges that remain. Preliminary investigations can form the basis for formal evaluations to continue to address gaps in knowledge.

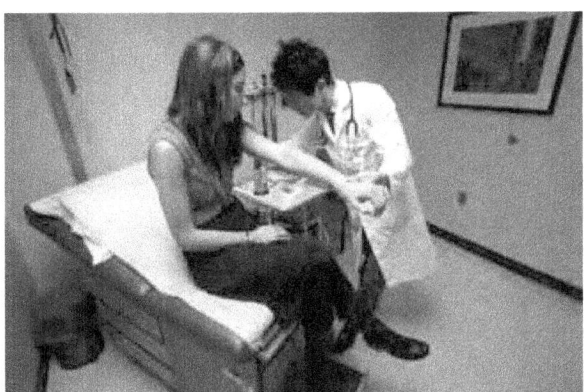

Evaluate Screening and Training Tools

Government agencies and private organizations developed a wealth of materials and resources to address human trafficking, although few were formally evaluated. Without evaluation, government and nongovernmental organizations are unable to establish the impact of these tools.

Federal agencies will work to coordinate efforts and resources to formally evaluate the effectiveness of these materials. Evaluated materials will be shared with the field to enhance the impact of their efforts.

➤ DOJ's National Institute of Justice will publish a client screening tool and user guide that were tested and evaluated by the Vera Institute of Justice to improve victim identification across diverse populations for use by victim service providers. DOJ's Office for Victims of Crime will provide the electronically published screening tool to all trafficking victim assistance grantees and the field.

➤ HHS will leverage the work of DOJ's National Institute of Justice to identify targeted screening tools for human trafficking for specific use within medical and health systems (including community clinics and emergency rooms), child welfare systems, mental health and substance abuse treatment providers, providers of services to homeless populations, human services programs, and other systems likely to encounter potential victims.

➤ HHS's Administration for Children and Families will explore the development of standardized health care protocols for intake (including increased focus on medical history and past intimate partner violence), evaluation/ examination, referrals, evidence collection, and long-term care (physical, oral, and mental) in human trafficking situations.

Improve the Quality of Evaluations

Government and nongovernmental organizations use a variety of outcome indicators and approaches to measure the impact of their efforts. This variety leads to a confusing array of inconsistent data and reports.

Federal agencies are committed to planning future outcome evaluations that will provide the baseline data and structure to be used for more rigorous evaluation efforts to support the development of evidence-based practices. Federal agencies will work in coordination with the Senior Policy Operating Group to better align performance metrics across Federal Government anti-human trafficking programs.

➤ DOJ's Office for Victims of Crime and HHS's Administration for Children and Families will convene a group of human trafficking victim service providers with the aim of identifying several performance measures that are commonly and effectively used to measure victim service outcomes.

• DOJ's Office for Victims of Crime and HHS's Administration for Children and Families will work with DOJ's National Institute of Justice to explore ways to develop technical assistance guides, tools, and templates for adaptation by a variety of human trafficking victim service providers to improve the effectiveness of their evaluation efforts.

• HHS's Administration for Children and Families will explore ways to leverage existing resources and performance metrics to evaluate the effectiveness of training curricula for stakeholders in the child welfare, runaway, and homeless youth systems.

• DOD will gauge the effectiveness of its combating trafficking in persons training by including several questions related to human trafficking in the *Status of Forces Survey*. This survey polls approximately 65,000 active duty and 80,000 reserve duty service members.

GOAL 3: EXPAND ACCESS TO SERVICES

Provide and promote outreach, training, and technical assistance to increase victim identification and expand the availability of services.

Unfortunately, too many people in the United States have either never heard of human trafficking or believe it is a crime that only occurs in foreign countries. Proactive efforts by government and nongovernmental entities to identify victims is critically important because the pervasive use of coercion, and the exploitation of victims' fears by perpetrators, leads few victims to seek assistance independently, either from law enforcement or service providers. Even when victims are identified, many first responders, including law enforcement and victim service providers at the federal, state, territorial, tribal, and local levels, remain unfamiliar with the range of services available to victims.[32] Public outreach to expand general awareness, and targeted training and technical assistance for allied professionals likely to encounter victims of human trafficking, is a crucial aspect of victim identification and coordinated service delivery. Improved understanding of human trafficking will allow individuals to identify victims and to provide them with referrals for the comprehensive array of services available to trafficking victims.

Federal agencies developed a variety of general awareness and targeted training materials based on their respective experience and expertise. Improved coordination and collaboration will allow for more effective and efficient development and distribution of information and materials, increasing the impact of these resources and awareness of human trafficking. Throughout the process of developing and updating outreach and training materials, efforts will be made to seek and incorporate feedback from survivors, victim service providers, anti-human trafficking organizations, and other subject matter experts.

To reach this goal, federal actions fall under two objectives:

OBJECTIVE 5: **Increase victim identification through coordinated public outreach and awareness efforts.**

OBJECTIVE 6: **Build capacity to better identify and serve victims through targeted training and technical assistance.**

OBJECTIVE 5:

Increase victim identification through coordinated public outreach and awareness efforts.

Federal partners, in coordination with the Senior Policy Operating Group, will collaborate on a comprehensive review of existing government public outreach and awareness materials and strategies and provide recommendations on increasing the effectiveness and efficiencies of these materials. In this review, federal partners will focus on materials designed for both the general public and for targeted audiences, distribution of materials, engagement of partners, and the development of new materials as appropriate. Federal agencies will work to make key public outreach and awareness materials more accessible by locating them on a common platform.

Conduct Outreach and Awareness Activities and Provide Resources for the General Public

The general public remains unaware of the breadth and depth of human trafficking in the United States. It is important that the general public becomes more aware of human trafficking in order to increase victim identification and referrals for service.

Federal agencies are engaged in a number of creative strategies to provide a special spotlight on human trafficking for the public. Agencies will share their strategies and work collaboratively on appropriate efforts to multiply the impact of their individual efforts. Federal agencies will collaboratively engage in special public outreach activities every January to highlight National Slavery and Human Trafficking Prevention Month.

Activities to highlight National Slavery and Human Trafficking Prevention Month

➤ DOJ's Office for Victims of Crime will create a public service announcement to raise the visibility of human trafficking. It will include survivor and stakeholder feedback to inform this effort and will explore providing the announcement in multiple languages.

➤ DHS's Blue Campaign will continue to hold a biannual stakeholder engagement event to coincide with National Slavery and Human Trafficking Prevention Month. This forum provides an opportunity to raise awareness of and solicit feedback on DHS's and its partners' efforts to combat human trafficking among the nongovernmental organization, faith-based, law enforcement, and government communities.

➤ The FBI's Office for Victim Assistance, in conjunction with National Slavery and Human Trafficking Prevention Month, will coordinate and participate in community

awareness events across the country, and include FBI resources on human trafficking at public venues such as libraries, community centers, and faith-based facilities by displaying books, posters, and other materials on human trafficking, slavery, and/or civil rights. These materials bring awareness to the warning signs of human trafficking, alert the public that it is a crime, and provide the National Human Trafficking Resource Hotline number.

➤ DOJ's Office of Community Oriented Policing Services will collaboratively engage in special public outreach activities every January to highlight National Slavery and Human Trafficking Prevention Month and will help promote guidance and promising practices identified and developed by other federal agencies via the Office of Community Oriented Policing Services Web site, e-mail blasts, Facebook posts, articles, and podcasts.

➤ HHS's Administration for Children and Families will coordinate with interested federal partners to strengthen engagement and awareness of human trafficking among youth through integration of youth-informed and youth-friendly prevention and intervention messages.

Tools and Resources

➤ DHS's Blue Campaign will create a public service announcement titled *Out of the Shadows,* which highlights the dangers of human trafficking and raises awareness of all forms of human trafficking.

➤ DHS's Blue Campaign will distribute new human trafficking awareness materials, including posters and a public service announcement, for the general public and groups likely to encounter victims.

➤ DHS's Blue Campaign and DOS's Office to Monitor and Combat Trafficking in Persons will collaborate to distribute awareness-raising materials to foreign embassies and consulates in the United States.

➤ DHS, HHS, and DOJ's Office for Victims of Crime will collaborate to develop and disseminate materials for national civic organizations comprised of state, territorial, tribal, and local governing leaders.

➤ DHS, HHS, and DOJ's Office for Victims of Crime will collaborate to develop and disseminate materials for national service organizations to educate their members about human trafficking, how to identify victims, and how to partner with local anti-human trafficking organizations.

➤ DOL and EEOC will continue to develop materials in multiple languages about basic rights to challenge employment discrimination, wage and hour violations, and similar employment issues. DOL and EEOC will coordinate with HHS's Administration for Children and Families and service providers to share these resources and information on the availability of such civil remedies.

TRAINING, OUTREACH, AND AWARENESS

While the focus of the Plan is on victim services, there is heavy emphasis on outreach, awareness, training, and technical assistance activities. Very few government agencies have the authority to include the development and provision of services to victims of human trafficking in their missions. For example, DOT is working hard to educate all of its employees and to collaborate with industry partners to increase identification of victims in transportation systems. Victim services, however, are not within the scope of DOT's mission and operations. Actions focused on outreach, awareness, training, and technical assistance highlight the range of government agencies that include human trafficking in their missions, as well as the importance of increasing general understanding of the crime as a necessary step leading to victim identification and access to services. Note that this Plan does not include all efforts related to human trafficking, as additional efforts focused on investigation and prosecution fall outside of the scope of the Plan.

SOME PRISON CELLS HAVE METAL BARS, AND SOME HAVE PICKET FENCES.

BLUE CAMPAIGN
One Voice. One Mission. End Human Trafficking.

Human trafficking is a global problem, and it's happening right here on Main Street, USA. Traffickers prey on the vulnerable, using trickery and coercion to imprison their victims into lives of domestic servitude. This is human trafficking, and it's a heinous crime. The Department of Homeland Security's *Blue Campaign* was created to turn the tables on those who sell human dignity for commercial gain. The Blue Campaign gives a unified voice to DHS agencies and their dedicated partners who combat human trafficking. Learn what you can do to help by visiting dhs.gov/bluecampaign.

For the purposes of the Plan and the action items detailed within, these terms are used to refer to the following related, but different, activities:

OUTREACH is defined as an action, carried out by an individual or organization, to contact and offer assistance to a person or community.

AWARENESS is defined as general information provided to a community or group to increase the knowledge or understanding of a subject, issue, or situation.

TRAINING is defined as an organized activity or process to impart information or instructions to improve the recipient's knowledge, attitudes, or skills needed to carry out a specific activity.

TECHNICAL ASSISTANCE is defined as targeted learning, usually between two people or within a small group. Technical assistance is generally less formal than training, often provided on demand and in response to ongoing cases or organizational issues.

➤ DHS's U.S. Immigration and Customs Enforcement Homeland Security Investigations will continue to distribute human trafficking brochures, pamphlets, posters, training videos, public service announcements, and human trafficking indicator cards. These materials will continue to be made available to field offices, law enforcement partners, nongovernmental organizations, and the general public, and will be available in multiple languages.

➤ DHS's U.S. Citizenship and Immigration Services will continue to distribute human trafficking brochures, one-pagers, human trafficking documentary videos, and other supporting Q&A documents. In addition to the current resources, U.S. Citizenship and Immigration Services will develop an instructional video for certifying officials pertaining to the certification process of both T and U visas. All resources will be available online and provided to stakeholders during training sessions.

➤ The FBI will continue to distribute human trafficking information and awareness materials, such as targeted cards, pamphlets, bookmarks, and other items that define and provide indicators of human trafficking. These materials will continue to be updated as needed, produced in multiple languages, and provided when meeting with law enforcement, service providers, and the general public.

➤ DOJ's U.S. Attorney's Office's Human Trafficking Task Forces will continue to provide public awareness and outreach on human trafficking through the creation of public service announcements, in-person training, forums, and other media, as necessary and within available resources. DOJ's Executive Office for United States Attorneys will enhance and ease the provision of such training through the creation of two training toolkits, one on labor trafficking and one on sex trafficking. The training toolkits will be distributed to U.S. Attorney's Office's trafficking points of contact, victim witness personnel, community outreach specialists, tribal liaisons, and law enforcement coordinators.

➤ DOS's Office to Monitor and Combat Trafficking in Persons will designate victim identification as the theme

of the *2013 Trafficking in Persons Report*, which forms the basis of the Office to Monitor and Combat Trafficking in Persons' diplomacy throughout the year, in order to highlight the global need to develop effective and careful victim identification criteria and approaches that result in the protection and restoration of victims.

➤ The FBI's Violent Crimes Against Children Section will continue to use a national billboard campaign, as well as bus board and bus stop ads, to increase awareness of trafficking of children and adults.

Web Sites and Social Media

➤ DOS's Office to Monitor and Combat Trafficking in Persons, in partnership with Slavery Footprint, will engage the general public and the private sector to raise awareness and increase demand for responsibly sourced goods and services by fostering consumers' understanding, action, and advocacy to encourage ethical sourcing practices by businesses. Response and activities will be measured through the Slavery Footprint platform.

➤ DHS's Blue Campaign, DOJ, DOS's Office to Monitor and Combat Trafficking in Persons, and HHS will expand human trafficking awareness efforts on social media, Twitter, and Facebook. DHS's Blue Campaign will also launch a redesigned Web site.

➤ EEOC will continue to update its Web site and social media feeds to educate the public that civil enforcement of the laws enforced by EEOC is an integral part of the fight against human trafficking. EEOC will also update human trafficking resources on its Web site.

Conduct Outreach and Awareness Activities and Provide Resources for Targeted Groups/ Communities

It is crucial that targeted outreach is provided to groups and communities that may encounter victims so they are able to identify victims and expand the network of services. These groups do not need to be experts in human trafficking; however, they need to have a general awareness and understanding of the indicators of the crime in order to provide needed referrals.

Federal agencies, in coordination with the Senior Policy Operating Group, will work collaboratively to deliver targeted outreach, including working to promote better awareness of existing tools, research, and information about labor trafficking. The development of materials and strategies will include interagency collaboration that will reduce redundancies and increase effectiveness.

Businesses and Employees

➤ DOL will implement a targeted public engagement campaign to disseminate its online toolkit for responsible businesses that wish to reduce child labor and forced labor in their supply chains, which includes information about victim referral mechanisms.

➤ DOL will share information and resources to raise awareness of trafficking among National Farmworker Jobs Program grantees.

➤ DOS's Bureau of Consular Affairs, with assistance from DHS's U.S. Citizenship and Immigration Services, will develop a Know Your Rights informational video to provide information on protections for certain employment- and education-based nonimmigrant visa applicants, including domestic workers. U.S. Embassies and Consulates overseas will play the video in waiting rooms as appropriate, in languages spoken by the greatest concentrations of those applicants.

➤ DOS, recognizing the vulnerabilities inherent in domestic work and the need to foreclose avenues of exploitation, particularly of those employed by diplomatic personnel, will continue its efforts to educate foreign mission personnel and their domestic workers about U.S. federal, state, and local laws, including protections for domestic workers employed by diplomatic personnel. The Department will periodically review its requirements and revise them as appropriate.

➤ DOS will develop procedures for the in-person registration of domestic workers employed by diplomatic personnel in the Washington, D.C., area shortly after their arrival in the United States to apprise them further of their rights and available services.

➤ HHS's Administration for Children and Families will identify opportunities to engage with businesses to post information on the National Human Trafficking Resource Center's Web site and to discuss possibilities for meeting the workforce development needs of survivors of human trafficking.

Housing Providers

➤ HUD will provide outreach and awareness materials to public housing agencies and Continuums of Care.

Medical Community

➤ HHS will collaborate through intra-agency efforts to develop and disseminate materials for public health organizations and associations.

Philanthropic Community

➤ DOJ's Office of Justice Programs will support a forum, in collaboration with a national philanthropic leader, to educate the philanthropic community about human trafficking and strategies to reduce demand for all forms of human trafficking, as well as the need for increased financial support through public/private partnerships.

Transportation Industry

➤ DHS and DOT will release the Blue Lightning Initiative, a human trafficking awareness training tailored to airline personnel. This training includes a computer-based training module and pocket guide on how to identify and report suspected human trafficking, in the air or on the ground, and how to notify federal law enforcement. DHS and DOT lead the initiative in coordination with and support from DHS's Human Smuggling and Trafficking Center, Federal Air Marshal Service, Federal Aviation Administration, nongovernmental organizations, and private industry. DHS's U.S. Customs and Border Protection and DOT will work to expand the reach of the Blue Lightning Initiative training to foreign-based airlines and aviation personnel after reviewing and assessing the initial release.

➤ DHS's Blue Campaign, DOT, and Amtrak will partner to train all 20,000 Amtrak employees and Amtrak police department officers to identify and recognize indicators of human trafficking, as well as how to report suspected cases of human trafficking.

➤ DOT will continue its work with stakeholders in the Transportation Leaders Against Human Trafficking partnership to encourage corporate participation, employee training, and public outreach campaigns across the transportation industry. DOT will create public awareness materials tailored for the transportation industry based on feedback from the partnership.

Youth

➤ DHS, DOJ's Office of Juvenile Justice and Delinquency Prevention, ED, and HHS's Administration for Children and Families will collaborate to develop and distribute materials for youth.

➤ DOL, in coordination with HHS's Administration for Children and Families, will share information and resources to raise awareness of trafficking among YouthBuild grantees.

➤ USAID will disseminate to students, scholars, and

> *"An important aspect of coordination and collaboration between agencies should be the development of a standardized training for agencies—one that is based on a uniform definition of human trafficking and then adapted to the specialized needs of each agency. Standardized trainings will help create more cohesion and unity between agencies."*
>
> – Coalition to Abolish Slavery and Trafficking

other stakeholders the research findings that result from its Counter-Trafficking Campus Challenge research grants that were awarded to the University of Southern California, Texas Christian University, and Vanderbilt University. The Campus Challenge included a Tech Challenge, a Research Competition, and an online community and education campaign (challengeslavery. org) to increase global awareness about human trafficking and to inspire activism among students and scholars at colleges and universities in the United States and abroad.

OBJECTIVE 6:

Build capacity to better identify and serve victims through targeted training and technical assistance.

Stakeholder feedback identified gaps in current training resources and emphasized the critical need for improved, coordinated, and ongoing training. Federal partners, in coordination with the Senior Policy Operating Group, will engage in ongoing discussions on how to catalog, share, and disseminate trainings to leverage resources, reduce duplication of efforts, and ensure needed trainings reach the intended audience.

Additionally, federal agencies will work proactively to ensure that human trafficking workshops and presentations are included on agendas of national conferences and training efforts, including conferences and trainings designed for law enforcement, victim service providers, tribal personnel, legal service providers, medical professionals, and mental health practitioners.

Expand Training of Federal Government Employees

Federal government employees are often in a position to identify human trafficking victims, but may not yet have the training needed to assist them effectively. Even those who do not interact with the public, if given the tools, can be a catalyst for change.

Agencies across the government will ensure that their personnel are well educated in human trafficking, are better able to identify victims, and can provide appropriate referrals for services.

Department of Agriculture

➤ USDA will make training on human trafficking available to all personnel.

Department of Defense

➤ DOD, in close collaboration with other agencies, will continue to update its law enforcement training, which focuses on victim identification, investigation, and information reporting and sharing with civilian or host nation law enforcement agencies. The updated training takes a scenario-based approach to training law enforcement professionals on understanding and ensuring victims' rights.

➤ The DOD Combating Trafficking in Persons program will continue to institute synchronized training, education, and outreach programs that ensure trafficking in persons awareness and support prevention, protection, and prosecution activities.

- DOD will continue to update its general awareness training, which all DOD civilian and military personnel are required to take. DOD will also create a 15-minute refresher training for those who have previously taken the longer training, as well as a training geared to contracting officers and acquisition personnel. Additionally, contractors likely to encounter victims of human trafficking will continue to be required to prove proficiency in human trafficking awareness before being awarded a contract.

- DOD will continue to collaborate with the American Forces Press Service and the Pentagon Channel to further educate troops through a targeted media campaign about how to identify victims and report human trafficking violations. The resulting media clips will highlight the Department's concentrated, internal efforts to train its members on human trafficking, as well as its accomplishments in human trafficking prevention, protection, and prosecution.

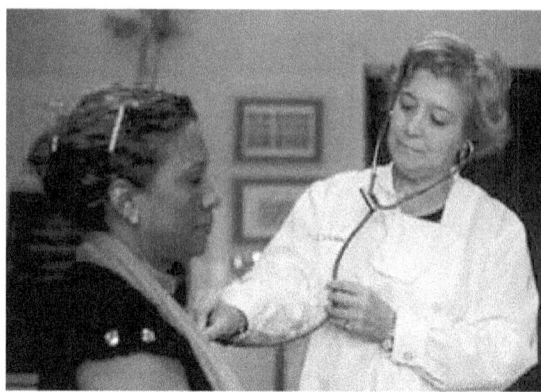

- DOD will continue to distribute awareness brochures, posters, and wallet-sized cards that explain workers' rights and provide hotline information to report suspected trafficking violations. These materials will continue to be posted around U.S. military bases to raise awareness among service members about workers' rights, as well as the penalties for engaging in human trafficking crimes.

Department of Health and Human Services

➤ HHS will provide guidance to its 10 regional offices on increasing strategic partnerships with state, territorial, tribal, and local governments and nongovernmental stakeholders for coordinated action to strengthen victim service systems.

➤ HHS will determine the appropriate personnel, and HHS-funded grantees and subcontractors, who should receive training on human trafficking and develop content and standards for that training. The training will be integrated as a standard requirement.

Department of Homeland Security

➤ DHS will continue to mandate that all of its employees who are likely to encounter victims of human trafficking take specialized training developed by DHS.

- All DHS U.S. Immigration and Customs Enforcement (ICE) personnel who are likely to encounter victims will complete mandatory human trafficking training. ICE will examine the feasibility of updating the training as necessary.

- ICE Homeland Security Investigations (ICE HSI) will provide periodic training to its subject matter experts on human trafficking. The training will focus on best practices involved in victim-centered investigations, including victim identification, provision of immigration benefits, and coordination with nongovernmental and faith-based organizations. The subject matter experts will continue to serve as designated points of contact regarding human trafficking and conduct general training to local law enforcement, nongovernmental organizations, and community groups.

- ICE HSI will conduct a 2-week advanced human smuggling and trafficking course at the Federal Law Enforcement Training Centers multiple times per year depending on funding availability.

- U.S. Citizenship and Immigration Services' (USCIS) public-facing employees are required to complete mandatory electronic-based human trafficking training. USCIS will consider adding to the training as needed.

- USCIS will provide periodic training on human trafficking and other related forms of immigration benefits to its community relations officers who provide outreach to stakeholders in their local districts on a range of topics.

- USCIS will continue to provide a training module on trafficking to all new officers at the USCIS Refugee, Asylum, and International Operations Directorate. Officers in the Asylum Division will receive additional training on mechanisms for referring potential victims of trafficking to ICE HSI when they apply for asylum, and how to share information with potential victims about trafficking-related immigration benefits.

- The U.S. Coast Guard will continue to maintain an online training provided by the DHS Blue Campaign on its training portal that is available to all its personnel, including those who may encounter victims of human trafficking. U.S. Coast Guard members represented on the DHS Blue Campaign will continue to evaluate and update the online training as needed.

- All U.S. Customs and Border Protection officers and agents, as part of Basic Training, will continue to receive information on what human trafficking is, how to detect it, and what to do upon an encounter. Incumbent officers and agents will continue to be required to complete the online Human Trafficking Awareness course annually.

- DHS's Federal Emergency Management Agency will continue to provide general awareness training to field-deployable employees to strengthen awareness, identification, and reporting of human trafficking.

➤ DHS will continue its outreach to DHS medical first responder personnel who are likely to encounter victims of human trafficking to encourage them to take specialized training developed by DHS.

- DHS's Office of Health Affairs and the Federal Emergency Management Agency will support outreach and training efforts to engage medical first responders to ensure they are able to identify and help potential victims.

- The Office of Health Affairs will coordinate with HHS to support outreach and training efforts to engage medical first responder personnel and hospital staff in emergency rooms and clinic environments.

➤ DHS and DOJ will coordinate cross training between federal law enforcement victim assistance specialists with federally funded service providers to enhance collaboration and coordination of services for trafficking victims.

Department of Justice

➤ The FBI will continue to provide various anti-human trafficking trainings and create additional training opportunities to foster increased awareness of human trafficking and identification of victims in the following ways:

- The FBI will train agents and victim specialists working in Indian Country on all aspects of human trafficking, specifically identifying and providing services for victims.

- The FBI will develop human trafficking awareness training for all its employees via the Virtual Academy training program.

- The FBI will continue to provide comprehensive human trafficking training to supervisors, agents, intelligence analysts, and victim specialists assigned to work on human trafficking matters. This training involves implementation of the FBI protocol for taking a victim-centered approach while conducting these investigations.

- The FBI's Violent Crimes Against Children Section will continue to provide in-person and online training regarding the protection of victims and use of the FBI Task Forces' resources in child sex trafficking investigations.

- The FBI will continue to provide training on the processes for supporting Continued Presence and T visa applications to all of its investigative personnel and victim specialists who work on human trafficking matters.

- The FBI will provide human trafficking training to additional DOJ entities, including the Drug Enforcement Administration, Bureau of Prisons, Bureau of Alcohol, Tobacco, Firearms and Explosives, and the U.S. Marshals Service. This training will include identifying and providing services to victims of human trafficking.

➤ DOJ's Executive Office for United States Attorneys will provide training on human trafficking resources, victim identification, and cultural sensitivity for victim-witness personnel.

Department of Labor

➤ DOL will make general awareness training available to all DOL personnel.

➤ DOL will finalize basic awareness and referral training for all Wage and Hour Division investigators. The training will be enhanced using stakeholder feedback, and subsequently made available to regional Occupational Safety and Health Administration management and their state counterparts for dissemination to enforcement staff.

➤ DOL will determine the appropriate DOL sub-agencies that should receive training on human trafficking and develop content and standards for that training.

Department of State

➤ DOS will make training on human trafficking available to all personnel.

➤ The Consular Training Division at DOS's Foreign Service Institute will continue to educate all new consular officers about the overseas adjudication of T and U visas for victims of trafficking and their qualifying family members, as well as the *Know Your Rights* (or Wilberforce) pamphlet. Consular officers are required to ensure that applicants of certain employment- and education-based visa categories read and understand the pamphlet, which is available in multiple languages.

➤ DOS's Foreign Service Institute will train mid-level officers on T and U visas to ensure managers have the tools necessary to address the complexity and sensitivity of these cases.

➤ The Visa Office will continue to train to its Public Inquiries Division on human trafficking to ensure that T and U visa cases are handled appropriately and receive the attention they deserve.

➤ DOS's Bureau of Diplomatic Security will create an online human trafficking investigation education course that includes instruction on how to identify and treat potential trafficking victims, the best practices to successfully investigate and prosecute trafficking offenses, and how to refer victims for services.

Department of Transportation

➤ DOT will train its employees on general human trafficking awareness.

U.S. Equal Employment Opportunity Commission

➤ Resources permitting, EEOC will determine the appropriate personnel who should receive training on human trafficking and develop content and standards for that training.

➤ Resources permitting, EEOC will work with its State Fair Employment Practices Agencies' counterparts to provide updates and training on labor trafficking issues.

U.S. Agency for International Development

➤ USAID will make training for all personnel on the Agency's Counter-Trafficking in Persons Code of Conduct mandatory; conduct counter-trafficking due diligence prior to awarding contracts, grants, and cooperative agreements; and respond to allegations of abuse.

Train and Assist State, Territorial, Tribal, and Local Law Enforcement and Criminal Justice Systems

The ability of law enforcement to effectively identify victims and hold offenders accountable depends on their capacity to connect with and support victims. It is also critically important that they know of services and immigration benefits available for victims of human trafficking.

Federal agencies are committed to collaboratively supporting law enforcement and criminal justice systems with improved and expanded training and technical assistance. Federal partners will work collaboratively, in coordination with the Senior Policy Operating Group, to improve the impact of individual training efforts.

General Training

➤ DHS and DOJ, supported by DOL and other federal partners, will develop common teaching points that are components of a victim-centered approach to human trafficking investigations. These topics will be integrated into the development and delivery of all trainings conducted by DHS and DOJ to federal, state, territorial, tribal, and local law enforcement agencies. Input from victim service providers and survivors will be included in the development of these points.

➤ DHS's U.S. Immigration and Customs Enforcement Homeland Security Investigations, Federal Law Enforcement Training Center, U.S. Citizenship and Immigration Services, and DOJ's Bureau of Justice

INTERSECTIONS OF HUMAN TRAFFICKING, CHILD WELFARE, AND JUVENILE JUSTICE

Federal agencies are aware of the intersection between child welfare and juvenile justice systems and human trafficking. Service providers and others who work with trafficking victims report that a significant percentage of trafficked minors have been involved in the child welfare and juvenile justice systems.[33] Risk factors, including maltreatment, poverty, instability, and the absence of a permanent, caring caregiver, make children vulnerable to human trafficking and to becoming involved in the child welfare and juvenile justice systems. The likelihood increases when their trauma is not identified, treated, and resolved. The Federal Government agencies that work most closely with the child welfare and juvenile justice systems (including HHS's Administration for Children and Families and DOJ's Office of Juvenile Justice and Delinquency Prevention) are working to improve their understanding of the causes and effective interventions to protect these children. Some specific activities are included in this Plan, but many more are in the planning stages and will be announced as they are finalized.

Assistance, Office of Juvenile Justice and Delinquency Prevention, Office for Victims of Crime, Office on Violence Against Women, and the FBI will coordinate to provide training and technical assistance resources, including roll call videos, training materials, and speakers, to national law enforcement membership organizations for their listservs, annual conferences, and victim service committees.

➤ DHS will continue to provide technical assistance to state, territorial, tribal, and local law enforcement organizations, first responder organizations, homeland security partners, Blue Campaign partners, and other targeted groups.

• DHS's U.S. Immigration and Customs Enforcement Homeland Security Investigations (ICE HSI), U.S. Citizenship and Immigration Services, Federal Law Enforcement Training Centers (FLETC) , and Office for Civil Rights and Civil Liberties will produce and distribute two short videos for federal, state, territorial, tribal, and local law enforcement that explain how immigration benefits (Continued Presence, T visas, and U visas) for victims of human trafficking can be beneficial to law enforcement investigations. These videos are designed to be shown to law enforcement officers at the roll call briefing that occurs before officers begin their shifts and will be publically available for anyone who works with law enforcement.

- ICE HSI and FLETC, pursuant to funding and resources, will continue to provide training and technical assistance to federal, state, territorial, tribal, and local law enforcement organizations and other targeted groups using DHS's law enforcement trainings as core training. FLETC will continue to work with state and local law enforcement to load DHS's Web-based state and local law enforcement human trafficking awareness training onto their statewide learning systems or use it in police academies. This interactive module introduces law enforcement officers to human trafficking and teaches them how to recognize indicators that someone may be a victim. This training could be supplemented by the state or locality to create a comprehensive approach to victim identification and highlight the importance of victim-centered practices.

- DHS, in coordination with the Senior Policy Operating Group, DOL, and EEOC, will endeavor to include a module on both labor trafficking and labor exploitation, including information on indicators and referral mechanisms, in the training it currently provides to local law enforcement through FLETC.

- ICE HSI and USCIS will continue to revise and deliver in-person and webinar training to federal, state, territorial, tribal, and local law enforcement and homeland security partners, as funding permits. Trainings will focus on how immigration benefits can support the stabilization and recovery of foreign national victims and further enhance rapport-building with victim-witnesses in human trafficking investigations.

- USCIS will produce a T visa resource guide for law enforcement. This will provide guidance on T visa basics, law enforcement's role in the T visa benefits, the T visa as a tool for law enforcement, a sample T visa declaration form, and frequently asked questions. Additionally, USCIS will continue to update and make available its *U Visa Resource Guide* as needed.

- DHS's Office of Health Affairs, Federal Emergency Management Agency, ICE HSI, and FLETC will continue to provide general awareness training of first responder communities through strategic partnerships to strengthen awareness, identification, and reporting of human trafficking.

- DHS Blue Campaign will increase distribution of its human trafficking awareness video and indicator cards tailored specifically for first responders. The

materials explain indicators of human trafficking that a first responder might encounter, what they can do to report suspected instances of human trafficking, and how to direct victims to services.

➤ DOT will continue to train about 6,000 state and local law enforcement officers across the country, including investigators at the Federal Motor Carrier Safety Administration, to detect human trafficking on trucks and buses.

➤ DOJ's Office of Community Oriented Policing Services, in partnership with the International Association of Chiefs of Police and the Yale Child Study Center, will develop a *Commercial Sexual Exploitation of Children Toolkit for Law Enforcement* to improve law enforcement's ability to recognize and respond to children through training, technical assistance, resource development, and information dissemination.

➤ The FBI will continue to conduct human trafficking investigative trainings for federal, state, territorial, tribal, and local law enforcement personnel as funding allows.

Task Forces

➤ DHS, DOJ, and DOL will continue to provide advanced human trafficking training for each Anti-Trafficking Coordination Team as funding allows.

➤ DOJ's Office for Victims of Crime will update and enhance the *Anti-Human Trafficking Task Force Strategy and Operations e-Guide* (https://www.ovcttac.gov/TaskForceGuide/EGuide/Default.aspx), providing updated guidance on collaboration, identification, prosecution, and service provision that is informed by federal partners and stakeholder feedback. A new section will be added on strategies for outreach and awareness.

➤ The FBI's Civil Rights Unit and Violent Crimes Against Children Section will continue to coordinate with the FBI's intelligence fusion cells to appropriately assess, rank, and address human trafficking threats throughout the United States to enhance the ability to locate and identify victims.

Tribal Law Enforcement

➤ DOJ's Bureau of Justice Assistance will design and deliver a human trafficking training to tribal law enforcement.

Criminal Justice Systems

➤ DHS, DOJ's Office of Juvenile Justice and Delinquency Prevention, and HHS's Administration for Children and Families will provide training materials about child trafficking to state juvenile justice agencies, juvenile justice specialists, State Advisory Group members, family and juvenile court judges and attorneys, public

"The training to increase collaboration with domestic violence, sexual assault, and stalking agencies mentioned in the plan should include education on the intersections of these issues with human trafficking and provision of services to human trafficking victims. Many of these agencies are already serving trafficking victims but need to feel incorporated into the anti-trafficking field not just as 'related fields' but as fields that have direct intersections with human trafficking and are filling the gaps in service provision throughout the country."

— Denver Anti-Trafficking Alliance, Denver District Attorney's Office

defenders, other juvenile justice system stakeholders, and others whose work includes providing direct services to child victims in residential and community-based programs in order to improve the states' responses to issues faced by child trafficking victims.

➤ The State Justice Institute will provide support to the Human Trafficking and the State Courts Collaborative, which will increase understanding and awareness about the challenges faced by state courts in dealing with cases involving trafficking victims and their families.

➤ Federal agencies will collaborate to expand the use and effectiveness of training for forensic interviews.

• DOJ's Office of Juvenile Justice and Delinquency Prevention, in collaboration with DHS's U.S. Immigration and Customs Enforcement Homeland Security Investigations' Victim Assistance Program, HHS's Administration for Children and Families, and the National Center for Missing and Exploited Children, will develop and deliver a curriculum on how to conduct forensic interviews with child victims of commercial sexual exploitation, including child victims of sex trafficking.

• DHS's U.S. Immigration and Customs Enforcement Homeland Security Investigations' Victim Assistance Program will explore the feasibility of increasing the number of forensic interviewers who can conduct legally defensible, victim-sensitive, and developmentally and culturally appropriate investigative interviews with victims of all ages and special populations.

➤ DOJ's Bureau of Justice Assistance will explore opportunities to continue to provide a training curriculum for state prosecutors on human trafficking developed by the Upper Midwest Policing Institute and the National Association of Attorneys General.

➤ DOJ's Bureau of Justice Assistance will continue to explore options, in consultation with the Office for Victims of Crime, to provide funding to train state and local law enforcement, prosecutors, and state judges on identifying trafficking and responding appropriately to victims.

Train and Assist Service Providers Working with Victims of Human Trafficking

Specialized anti-human trafficking service providers and those who work with human trafficking victims on a regular basis provide critical assistance and care to victims to ensure their needs are met in the immediate aftermath of the crime, as well as throughout their long-term recovery. These service providers are leaders in the anti-human trafficking field, helping to inform federal efforts.

Federal agencies will continue to provide training and technical assistance to these key partners to support and enhance the quality and effectiveness of services provided.

Capacity Building Efforts

➤ DOJ's Office for Victims of Crime, the FBI, DOL, and HHS's Administration for Children and Families will provide training and technical assistance to anti-human trafficking organizations on developing relationships with business, labor, philanthropic, and health care leaders via training forums and materials.

➤ DOJ's Office for Victims of Crime and Bureau of Justice Assistance, in collaboration with HHS's Administration for Children and Families, will host a Regional Training Forum, subject to DOJ budgetary approval, bringing together Anti-Human Trafficking Task Forces with investigative and victim service functions to discuss case information, share intelligence, and network with law enforcement and service providers in order to foster greater linkages and emphasize the importance of a coordinated, multidisciplinary response to human trafficking. If approval is not provided, the Office for Victims of Crime will host a series of webinars to present Regional Training Forum workshop topics.

➤ DOS's Bureau of Diplomatic Security will continue to educate the nongovernmental community about its ability to identify victims of human trafficking, domestically and overseas, and work on trafficking cases, particularly those related to visa fraud and the foreign diplomatic community.

➤ DHS's U.S. Immigration and Customs Enforcement Homeland Security Investigations' Victim Assistance Program, DOJ's Office for Victims of Crime and Office on Violence Against Women, and HHS's Administration for Children and Families and Substance Abuse and Mental Health Services Administration will partner to develop and provide training support in the form of webinars and conference sessions on the impact of trauma and polyvictimization[34] on victims and the need for trauma-informed care to grantees, law enforcement-based victim specialists, and other service providers. Developing additional partnerships will broaden the scope and impact of this effort over time.

➤ DOJ's Office of Juvenile Justice and Delinquency Prevention and HHS's Administration for Children and Families will partner to offer training on gender-specific services to providers working with child victims.

➤ DOJ's Office of Juvenile Justice and Delinquency Prevention will provide targeted training and technical assistance to AMBER Alert coordinators, child abduction response teams, missing children clearinghouses, and other state, territorial, tribal, and local partners who recover child abduction victims.

➤ DHS's U.S. Immigration and Customs Enforcement Homeland Security Investigations' Victim Assistance Program and U.S. Citizenship and Immigration Services will continue to conduct, as funding allows, trainings and presentations for federal, state, territorial, tribal, and local law enforcement, nongovernmental organizations, attorneys, judges, and others on combating human trafficking and available immigration benefits for victims of human trafficking.

➤ HHS's Administration for Children and Families will provide guidance on safe and ethical victim outreach practices in coordination with DOJ and DHS.

➤ DOJ's Office for Victims of Crime will produce a new human trafficking training video that highlights appropriate and culturally competent services for various victim populations.

➤ DOJ's Office for Victims of Crime will provide access to training in trauma-informed care practices to its anti-human trafficking program grantees.

➤ DOJ's Office for Victims of Crime will provide its anti-human trafficking grantees with training and technical assistance on supporting victims of human trafficking in accessing services needed to attain financial stability and independence.

Train and Assist the Broader Victim Services Field

Public and nonprofit victim service providers have experience, expertise, and resources that should be better integrated with federal anti-human trafficking efforts.

Federal agencies will develop training and enhance collaborative efforts to better integrate these sectors, create linkages between systems, increase victim identification, and expand and improve the services provided to victims of human trafficking. When developing and updating new training resources, agencies will make efforts to seek and incorporate feedback from survivors, victim service providers, and other stakeholders.

General Victim Service Providers

➤ HHS will provide training resources on human trafficking to grantees in relevant refugee resettlement, child welfare, runaway and homeless youth, domestic violence, and tribal communities.

➤ DOJ's Office for Victims of Crime will provide targeted training and technical assistance on human trafficking and capacity building for Victims of Crime Act victim assistance administrators at annual conferences.

➤ DOJ's Office for Victims of Crime will review the Victim Assistance Training Online and the National Victim Assistance Academy curricula and add information on human trafficking where appropriate.

➤ DOJ's Office for Victims of Crime will support a workshop at the 30th National Symposium on Child Abuse, a premier conference that provides expert training to professionals in the child maltreatment field. The workshop will define and connect the issues of child sexual abuse, human trafficking, and commercial sexual exploitation of children, highlighting the important role Child Advocacy Centers can play in victim identification and service provision.

➤ DOJ's Office for Victims of Crime will extend outreach and collaboration efforts to ensure that its resources, such as the *Supporting Crime Victims with Disabilities* instructor-led training and *Promising Practices to Serving Victims with Disabilities Toolkit,* are available to practitioners who may encounter persons with disabilities who are at risk of being trafficked. The Office for Victims of Crime will modify its *Supporting Crime Victims with Disabilities* training to incorporate content on the dynamics of human trafficking and the intersection of trafficking with persons with disabilities.

➤ As part of its update and enhancement efforts to the *Anti-Human Trafficking Task Force Strategy and Operations e-Guide*, DOJ's Office for Victims of Crime will include specific content and resources on trafficking of persons with disabilities, including promising practices on investigation of these cases and service provision that is fully accessible and culturally appropriate.

➤ The FBI will continue to provide trainings with and to victim service providers, community leaders, faith-based organizations, and other nongovernmental organizations as funding allows.

- DHS's Federal Law Enforcement Training Center will continue to enhance and expand training and technical assistance to federal, state, territorial, tribal, local, private, and nongovernmental entities seeking to create training on the indicators of human trafficking, and how to work with federal law enforcement in the provision of victim assistance in human trafficking cases, as funding allows.

- DHS's U.S. Immigration and Customs Enforcement Homeland Security Investigations and U.S. Citizenship and Immigration Services will continue to revise and deliver in-person and webinar trainings to victim service providers and immigration attorneys as funding allows. Trainings will focus on how certain immigration benefits can support the stabilization and recovery of eligible victims and will explain the application process for such benefits.

Domestic Violence and Sexual Assault Providers

- HHS's Administration for Children and Families Family and Youth Services Bureau will provide targeted training on human trafficking for Family Violence Prevention and Services Act Program State Administrators and Tribal Grantees, as well as State Domestic Violence Coalitions at annual grantee meetings.

- HHS's Administration for Children and Families and DOJ's Office for Victims of Crime and Office on Violence Against Women will provide annual training and technical assistance (which may include webinars, workshops, and/or training materials) on the intersections of human trafficking, domestic violence, and sexual assault.

- HHS's Administration for Children and Families will offer at least one training and technical assistance webinar for domestic violence victim service providers based on the Asian Pacific Islander Institute on Domestic Violence's *Considerations and Recommendations for Battered Women's Advocates* technical assistance brief.

- DOJ's Office on Violence Against Women will expand collaboration at the local level among its grantees and stakeholders in the domestic violence, sexual assault, and anti-human trafficking fields by providing national training that incorporates multidisciplinary teams from different localities.

- DOJ's Office on Violence Against Women will provide at least one webinar for its grantees on how to identify and respond to domestic minor sex trafficking and how to collaborate with anti-human trafficking organizations and organizations that serve vulnerable youth.

Train and Assist Allied Professionals

Human trafficking is a crime that often intersects with other crimes. Although it is usually hidden, some victims encounter medical professionals, teachers, public safety officials, and others who could potentially assist the victim in escaping into freedom.

Federal agencies will provide human trafficking training and technical assistance to public and private agencies that may encounter victims of human trafficking through their work with victims of other crimes and vulnerable populations to increase victim identification and leverage resources.

Education Systems

- ED will provide information to school communities with the goal of raising awareness and engaging school staff in prevention, victim identification, and victim support. DHS, the FBI, ED, and HHS's Administration for Children and Families will partner to raise awareness of human trafficking on school campuses.

  - ED will develop a guide to raise awareness in school communities about the commercial sexual exploitation of students, including child sex trafficking, and how to identify and support student victims. ED will continue to partner with school districts that commit to addressing and reducing human trafficking on campuses. ED will assist districts in raising awareness, suggesting partners that will support those efforts, offering model reporting protocols, and making training and resources available. ED's work with these districts can be a model for replication.

  - DHS, ED, and HHS's Administration for Children and Families, upon availability of funding, will develop and disseminate training materials and resources for school staff and administrators.

  - ED will work with DHS to disseminate products co-branded with the Blue Campaign for use in and by schools.

- HHS's Administration for Children and Families, in conjunction with other HHS components, will explore possibilities of partnering with social work schools, counseling schools, and related professional associations to increase training for social work and health professionals on meeting the needs of human trafficking victims.

- HHS's Administration for Children and Families will explore training opportunities for family service workers in Head Start programs to identify, serve, and provide referrals to victims of human trafficking.

- HHS's Administration for Children and Families and Health Resources and Services Administration will consider strategies, in coordination with intra- and interagency partners, to raise awareness about human trafficking in community colleges.

"The public benefits available to a human trafficking victim may vary on a case-by-case basis. Due to the complexities in meeting the eligibility requirements for these programs, victims are generally unable to obtain public benefits on their own. Legal aid providers and victim services agencies help trafficking victims access public benefits and meet their basic survival needs, but they often lack the funding and staff capacity to fully meet this need."

– Santa Clara University Law School

Faith-Based and Community-Based Organizations

➤ DHS's Center for Faith-based and Neighborhood Partnerships and U.S. Immigration and Customs Enforcement Homeland Security Investigations' Victim Assistance Program will conduct and evaluate a pilot training and technical assistance initiative for faith-based and other neighborhood community-based organizations. The initiative will engage clergy and community leaders so they can educate their communities about human trafficking, identify vulnerable persons, and develop practical strategies and action steps to encourage congregants and other local leaders to respond to the needs of human trafficking victims.

➤ DHS's Center for Faith-based and Neighborhood Partnerships and U.S. Immigration and Customs Enforcement Homeland Security Investigations' Victim Assistance Program will conduct training and technical assistance initiatives for faith-based and other neighborhood community-based organizations in two cities per year that have a high incidence of human trafficking. They will also collaborate with other federal partners, including DOJ's Office for Victims of Crime, DOL, HHS's Administration for Children and Families, and HUD, to disseminate the materials and implement the strategies developed. These initiatives are contingent on the evaluation of the pilot and available funding.

Labor and Employment Systems

➤ DOL, in coordination with DOJ and HHS, will provide updated training on trafficking issues to the State Farmworker Monitor Advocates.

➤ DOL will deliver two webinar trainings to the public workforce system that highlight promising practices in employment and training services.

Health Care Systems

➤ HHS will engage health care provider organizations to educate the health care community about human trafficking and to increase services and support for victims.

➤ HHS will provide guidance on addressing major gaps in medical treatment and services for victims of human trafficking, as well as sensitivity and cultural competency training to decrease stigma associated with human trafficking. HHS will explore the possibility and process of expanding hospital codes, such as International Classification of Diseases 10 or Diagnostic and Statistical Manual of Mental Disorders, to allow for better reflection of cost of care and time spent on these cases. These codes do not currently include an option for human trafficking cases.

➤ HHS's Administration for Children and Families will form a technical working group of health care professionals, including physicians, nurses, and community health practitioners, to identify opportunities for increased training and collaboration to better identify and serve victims within targeted health systems. The Administration for Children and Families will then provide recommendations for training on identifying victims of human trafficking and how to meet their physical and mental health needs.

GOAL 4: IMPROVE OUTCOMES

Promote effective, culturally appropriate, trauma-informed services that improve the short- and long-term health, safety, and well-being of victims.

Victims of human trafficking require a multidisciplinary response to address fully the impact of their victimization. Service providers express concern at the lengthy and confusing process of connecting victims with available services. Through the public comment period, nongovernmental organizations also reported that additional resources, from both government and nongovernmental sources, are needed to provide comprehensive long-term victim care, including health care and key legal services.[35] Victims would also benefit from access to varying services depending on their specialized needs, and it may be challenging for service providers to meet those needs for the length of time it takes to stabilize a victim.[36]

Federal agencies will work together and coordinate with state, territorial, tribal, and local governments to create a more efficient service delivery system that is accessible and responsive to the needs of all identified victims of human trafficking.

To reach this goal, federal actions fall under two objectives:

OBJECTIVE 7: Foster collaborations and partnerships to enhance the community response to human trafficking.

OBJECTIVE 8: Improve access to victim services by removing systemic barriers.

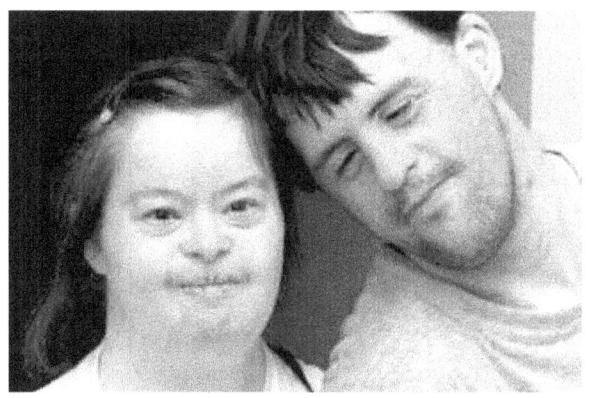

OBJECTIVE 7:

Foster collaborations and partnerships to enhance the community response to human trafficking.

Federal agencies will develop stronger and more effective collaborations with community-based organizations, including those from cultural, ethnic, and religious communities, in order to increase victim identification and improve victim services. Federal agencies will focus their resources on supporting the growth and development of sustainable local providers who are best able to tailor their work to the needs of the immediate community.

Develop Networks to Increase Identification of Victims of Human Trafficking

Human trafficking exists in a wide range of settings and communities. Partnerships must be equally wide ranging and diverse in response. Strategies to address the identification of underserved populations require tactical collaborations with nontraditional partners.

Federal agencies will work to identify new and expanded partnerships that are likely to uncover human trafficking. Partnerships with these organizations will expand the victim service network and increase victim identification, particularly among vulnerable populations.

General Partnerships

➤ HHS will work with partners, and relevant HHS-funded grantees and contractors, in the medical, educational, and other stakeholder communities to identify trends in human trafficking of service-related professionals, including elder care providers and teachers.

➤ HHS will identify opportunities to reach out to community partners who can aid in victim identification, including health care providers, unions, and housing authorities

and inspectors who may have contact with potential victims of human trafficking.

➤ DOD will partner with government agencies, external stakeholders, nongovernmental organizations, and the private sector to make trainings more victim-centered and ensure troops know where to refer victims for assistance.

➤ The FBI will continue to coordinate its anti-human trafficking efforts through partnerships with various hotels and medical facilities, and in trainings provided at Citizens Academies. These partnerships and trainings will provide increased awareness that may lead to further victim identification.

➤ The FBI will foster greater relationships with juvenile detention facility personnel.

➤ The FBI's Office for Victim Assistance will establish public-private partnerships using victim specialist outreach in local communities.

➤ DOJ's U.S. Attorney's Office Human Trafficking Task Forces will continue to partner with nonprofit organizations and federal, state, territorial, tribal, and local agencies to combat and increase awareness of trafficking, as appropriate and within available resources.

➤ DHS's U.S. Immigration and Customs Enforcement Homeland Security Investigations will continue to develop existing partnerships while also establishing new partnerships with community groups, law enforcement, nongovernmental organizations, private industry, faith-based service providers, immigrant community-based organizations, adult club industry affiliates, financial institution partners, and local and federal regulatory agencies.

➤ DHS's Blue Campaign will continue to pursue formal co-branding partnerships with a range of groups, such as businesses, private sector, hotels, government associations, medical and first responder organizations, and law enforcement. Through these partnerships, materials and resources are shared with both the private and public sector.

"I think that providing low barrier access to services and better identification of victims and survivors so they can access services is really the key to responding to human trafficking. I think that focusing on this gives us a more actionable plan than spreading ourselves too broadly."

– International Rescue Committee Washington

➤ EEOC will continue to work on targeted outreach and expansion of significant partnerships with stakeholder organizations involved in the fight against human trafficking. EEOC will continue to work toward protecting the rights of victims of human trafficking, who are prioritized as a class of vulnerable workers.

American Indian/Alaska Native Communities

➤ The FBI will broaden its community outreach efforts within American Indian/Alaska Native communities throughout the United States to include law enforcement agencies, community leaders, and social service providers.

➤ HHS will incorporate the topic of human trafficking in ongoing tribal consultations and identify information distribution channels to relevant programs through HHS's Indian Health Service.

➤ DHS's Office of Health Affairs will coordinate tribal outreach through emergency medical associations with tribal affiliations.

Faith-based and Community-based Organizations

➤ DOJ's U.S. Attorney's Office Human Trafficking Task Forces will continue to partner with faith-based and community-based organizations to improve victim identification and services.

➤ DHS's U.S. Immigration and Customs Enforcement Homeland Security Investigations' Victim Assistance Program and the FBI's victim specialists and community outreach specialists will continue to participate on human trafficking and FBI Child Exploitation Task Forces to develop partnerships with faith-based, cultural, ethnic, and other local community-based organizations. These partnerships will increase victim identification and forward prevention efforts.

Labor and Employment Systems

➤ DOL, EEOC, and HHS will leverage relationships with domestic worker, farmworker, guest worker, worker centers, workers' advocacy organizations, and other labor organizations to identify opportunities for victim identification and/or connection to services through the National Human Trafficking Resource Center.

Runaway and Homeless Youth Systems

➤ HHS's Administration for Children and Families will work with runaway and homeless youth programs to identify opportunities for victim identification in human trafficking networks related to exploitative peddling operations, which often take the form of youth selling food items, produce, flowers, inexpensive household products, used merchandise, and fix-it services.

➤ ED will work with the National Center for Homeless Education to make anti-human trafficking resources, such as webinars and relevant materials, available to its membership.

Develop Networks to Expand Access to Services

Victims of human trafficking have a wide range of needs and experiences. Networks and partnerships with organizations that serve populations at risk for trafficking, such as child welfare, runaway and homeless youth services, sexual assault and domestic violence services, immigration services, and migrant worker support networks, need to expand to provide appropriate services and referrals for victims of human trafficking.

Federal agencies will collaborate with a diverse array of partners who offer services, support, or access that can address the needs of victims.

Comprehensive Victim Services

➤ DOJ's Office for Victims of Crime and Office of Juvenile Justice and Delinquency Prevention, DOS's Office to Combat and Monitor Trafficking in Persons, HHS's Administration for Children and Families, and HUD will engage with Humanity United, as appropriate, in a public-private capacity-building initiative to identify innovative solutions to key gaps in victim services.

➤ DHS, DOJ, and HHS's Administration for Children and Families will coordinate and streamline efforts to use victim assistance law enforcement and prosecution-based specialists to help connect victims to appropriate services, including housing, medical and mental health support, and legal representation, including immigration assistance.

Employment and Financial Stability

➤ DOJ's Office for Victims of Crime, DOL, and HHS's Administration for Children and Families will continue to strengthen and participate in an informal network of grantee organizations, local and state workforce investment boards, and stakeholder groups around the issue of employment and training services for victims of trafficking. The network will continue to build upon initial listening sessions by sharing and promoting, where possible, the integration of information about underutilized services into service delivery, common barriers to employment, and promising practices in employment and training services.

➤ HHS's Administration for Children and Families will explore the possibility of engaging its Assets for Independence program to provide support for survivors of human trafficking.

➤ DOL and HHS's Administration for Children and Families will facilitate discussions and relationships among community-based organizations and business communities and industries to support components of victim service programs, including information on employment and training services and workforce development efforts.

Families and Youth Support

➤ DOJ's Office of Juvenile Justice and Delinquency Prevention will expand evidence-based mentoring initiatives to develop specific outreach to child victims and provide training to mentoring experts, and consider ways to build partnerships among national mentoring organizations and local programs serving child victims of sexual exploitation, including sex trafficking.

➤ DOJ's Office for Victims of Crime will provide additional guidance to its anti-human trafficking grantees on the provision of services to family members of victims of human trafficking.

➤ ED will collaborate with federal partners to strengthen coordination among, and provide guidance to, its migrant youth programs, runaway and homeless youth programs, and other relevant programs.

➤ ED will develop at least one webinar for school community grantees on how to identify and respond to minor sex trafficking and how to collaborate with organizations that serve vulnerable youth.

OBJECTIVE 8:

Improve access to victim services by removing systemic barriers.

Federal agencies are committed to identifying effective approaches to reduce and remove barriers to ensure that victims of human trafficking have access to the full range of services they need. Special efforts will be made to identify the needs of vulnerable populations and to ensure they have equal access to services and support.

Improve Access to Services and Benefits

Human trafficking victims often struggle to access the full range of benefits and services that would address their needs. Immigration status, access to identity documents, poverty, limited education and job skills, and medical and mental health problems are among the issues that must be addressed to support victims.

Federal agencies will work collaboratively, in coordination with the Senior Policy Operating Group, to improve the services and benefits provided to victims. Policies, practices, procedures, and funding mechanisms will be reviewed.

Housing

➤ HHS's Administration for Children and Families will review how current policies, practices, regulations, and statutes guiding runaway and homeless youth and domestic violence shelters either inhibit or allow for housing and residence of human trafficking victims and consider strategies to remove barriers, including statutory or regulatory changes.

"One of the primary barriers we face as service providers is finding appropriate housing for survivors, especially transitional/emergency housing. Not having safe, affordable housing to turn to means that victims are more likely to stay in exploitative situations (because there is nowhere else to go), or be re-trafficked or otherwise unsafe. Even if we manage to find safe housing, there is a risk of wiping out their entire services fund to pay rent and not having enough left over for other basic needs."

– Break the Chain Campaign

➤ HHS's Administration for Children and Families will identify partnership opportunities with HUD and youth providers to review federal policies regarding homelessness and requirements that may prevent victims of human trafficking from qualifying for available housing.

➤ HHS's Administration for Children and Families will review how policies affecting youth aging out of foster care impact victims of human trafficking and explore possibilities to recruit and train specialized foster parents to care for survivors of human trafficking.

➤ HHS's Administration for Children and Families will explore public-private partnerships with businesses, philanthropic foundations, and faith-based and other community-based organizations and leaders to support ongoing housing needs.

➤ DOJ's Office for Victims of Crime will collaborate with HHS's Administration for Children and Families, HUD, and DOJ components the National Institute of Justice and the Office on Violence Against Women to evaluate the appropriateness and feasibility of housing demonstration projects, including single-site and subsidized housing plans.

➤ DHS's U.S. Immigration and Customs Enforcement Homeland Security Investigations' Victim Assistance Program, the FBI's Office for Victim Assistance, and DOJ's U.S. Attorneys' Offices, through their field-based victim assistance specialists, will make referrals to local service provider organizations to provide appropriate housing options for human trafficking victims identified in federal investigations and prosecutions. In the absence of any emergency housing, U.S. Immigration and Customs Enforcement Homeland Security Investigations' Victim Assistance Program and the FBI's Office for Victim Assistance may consider using Federal Emergency Victim Assistance funds as a last resort until an appropriate housing option is available.

Comprehensive Legal Services

➤ DOJ's Office for Victims of Crime (OVC) will engage in a multi-year, multi-pronged effort to build capacity for legal services for all crime victims, including victims of human trafficking, called *Legal Assistance for Crime Victims: An OVC Capacity Building Initiative*. The initiative will provide training and technical assistance for pro bono and low-cost legal service providers to expand their services to victims of human trafficking.

➤ DOJ's Office for Victims of Crime will continue to explore ways to support and strengthen the current Wraparound Victim Legal Assistance Network Demonstration Project grants, which create partnerships that provide comprehensive legal services to crime victims.

➤ DOJ's Office for Victims of Crime and Office on Violence Against Women, and HHS's Administration for Children and Families, with the assistance of DOJ's Access to Justice Initiative, will explore opportunities to leverage existing federal resources, including available training and technical assistance, to partner with the Legal Services Corporation and other legal services providers to provide training on the identification of human trafficking victims and to support the provision of comprehensive legal services.

➤ DOJ's Office for Victims of Crime and Office on Violence Against Women, and HHS's Administration for Children and Families, will continue to provide grant funding to support legal services and will collaborate to develop and provide training and technical assistance (including written guidance, webinars, conferences, and training materials) to grantees and other providers on the remedies available to victims of human trafficking.

- DHS's U.S. Immigration and Customs Enforcement Homeland Security Investigations' Victim Assistance Program, the FBI's Office for Victim Assistance, and DOJ's U.S. Attorneys' Offices, through their field-based victim assistance specialists, will make referrals to appropriate legal service providers for human trafficking victims identified in federal investigations and prosecutions, including for legal services related to immigration and family law.

Immigration Benefits

- DHS is committed to updating its regulations to streamline the application process and provide clearer guidance on how to obtain T nonimmigrant status, while also ensuring the integrity of the immigration system.

- DHS's U.S. Immigration and Customs Enforcement Homeland Security Investigations, the FBI's Office for Victim Assistance, and DOJ's U.S. Attorneys' Offices, through their field-based victim assistance specialists, will identify human trafficking victims in federal investigations and prosecutions who may be eligible for immigration benefits and assist in the coordination of Continued Presence, law enforcement certifications for the T or U nonimmigrant visas, and referrals to immigration attorneys to provide further assistance to victims.

ADDRESSING THE NEEDS OF VULNERABLE POPULATIONS

Federal agencies are aware that there are specific populations, including rural victims, men and boys, American Indians and Alaska Natives, and the lesbian, gay, bisexual, transgender, and questioning community, whose unique needs are not being addressed adequately. These populations require more attention and focus to ensure understanding of their vulnerabilities and needs so that responses are effective. The Federal Government acknowledges that it currently does not have enough information on human trafficking and service provision to these vulnerable populations to begin making recommendations to the field. Federal agencies are committed to spending the time and resources needed during the period of this Plan to learn enough to chart the course forward.

- DHS's U.S. Citizenship and Immigration Services and U.S. Immigration and Customs Enforcement Homeland Security Investigations will continue to train law enforcement and immigration attorneys on Continued Presence and T and U visas and to facilitate understanding of the application process, including the role of law enforcement and the certification process.

- DHS's U.S. Citizenship and Immigration Services will provide training to adjudicators of T and U visas at the Vermont Service Center to ensure a comprehensive understanding of human trafficking, particularly in light of evolving and changing trends, as needed.

- The Vermont Service Center of DHS's U.S. Citizenship and Immigration Services will provide information and resources to the Fraud Detection and National Security units about suspect companies, employers, and recruiters that are identified during the adjudication of the T visa to prevent further exploitation of the immigration process.

- DHS will continue to identify and assist victims through its U.S. Immigration and Customs Enforcement Homeland Security Investigations by issuing Continued Presence for qualified victims, providing referrals to HHS, and issuing employment authorization documents through U.S. Citizenship and Immigration Services, as appropriate.

- DOL, a certifying agency for U visas, with assistance from DHS's U.S. Citizenship and Immigration Services, will explore the feasibility of completing law enforcement declarations for T visas. DOL will engage with stakeholder groups around the issues permitting or preventing such expansion.

- EEOC, a certifying agency for U visas, with assistance from DHS's U.S. Citizenship and Immigration Services, will examine whether it can play a similar role with respect to T visas and, if so, will develop policies and protocols to do so.

Victim Compensation Programs

- DOJ's Office for Victims of Crime will work to increase access to crime victim compensation for human trafficking victims through policy clarification, focused information, and training and technical assistance to state Victims of Crime Act compensation program administrators.

Increase Access for Vulnerable Populations

Perpetrators of human trafficking often exploit the limited English proficiency of their victims. Human traffickers can also target people with physical, mental, sensory, and developmental disabilities. Additionally, some victims develop mental and physical conditions due to their exploitation by traffickers. It is critical that first responders, service providers, government agencies, and others are able to communicate directly, clearly, and accurately with victims and provide appropriate auxiliary aids and services.

Federal agencies will continue to ensure that all federally administered and funded programs comply with civil rights requirements and work to better identify and share policies, procedures, tools, and technology to improve access in the anti-human trafficking field.

"Our Nation was founded on the enduring principles of equality and freedom for all. As Americans, it is our solemn responsibility to honor and uphold this legacy."

— President Barack Obama, December 22, 2010

Victims with Limited English Proficiency

➤ HHS's Administration for Children and Families will provide a directory of language access options available through service providers and identify innovative uses of technology to provide language access to victims. HHS's Office for Civil Rights will provide technical assistance so that the Administration for Children and Families can continue to make grant recipients aware of their obligations to provide language assistance.

➤ DHS will continue to provide language identification tools, known as the I-Speak materials, which were modified by its Office for Civil Rights and Civil Liberties and the Blue Campaign to fit the human trafficking context, to DHS and law enforcement entities for use in identifying the language of victims and to enhance communication through appropriate interpretation services. The tools will be made available to the public on the DHS Blue Campaign Web site, and DHS will distribute hard copies to DHS personnel who are likely to encounter victims of human trafficking.

➤ DHS's Office for Civil Rights and Civil Liberties will work to translate the Blue Campaign awareness products into multiple languages to increase the accessibility of information about the signs of human trafficking and the resources available to human trafficking victims.

➤ EEOC will work with its language access officers and other employees, as appropriate, to ensure that they are familiar with current trends and signs of human trafficking.

➤ DOJ's U.S. Attorney's Office victim-witness personnel will continue to utilize available resources to ensure that human trafficking victims with limited English proficiency can participate meaningfully in federal prosecutions.

Victims with Disabilities

➤ HHS will promote policies, training, and outreach efforts to ensure victims with disabilities receive necessary auxiliary aids and services in order to meaningfully participate in programs and receive services. HHS's Office for Civil Rights will provide technical assistance so that HHS can continue to make grant recipients aware of their obligations to provide auxiliary aids and services.

➤ HHS's Administration for Children and Families will explore public-private partnerships with advocacy groups, foundations, businesses, and faith-based and other community-based groups to support the needs of victims who have disabilities.

➤ DHS's U.S. Immigration and Customs Enforcement Homeland Security Investigations will continue to support forensic interviewers who can conduct legally defensible, victim sensitive, developmentally and culturally appropriate investigative interviews with victims of all ages and special populations, including victims with disabilities.

➤ DHS's Office for Civil Rights and Civil Liberties will continue to work to ensure full inclusion and equal access for all persons with disabilities who interact with DHS, including victims of trafficking, under federal civil rights laws. The effort includes providing coordination and guidance to DHS components regarding their federally conducted activities as well as for recipients of DHS financial assistance.

➤ The FBI's Office for Victim Assistance will provide training to FBI personnel on considerations for working with human trafficking victims with disabilities.

➤ Resources permitting, EEOC will consider the development of outreach and training materials to address issues involving trafficking of individuals with disabilities.

APPENDIX A: ACRONYMS

Department of Justice (DOJ) Entities

BJA – Office of Justice Programs, Bureau of Justice Assistance
COPS - Community Oriented Policing Services
EOUSA - Executive Office for United States Attorneys
FBI – Federal Bureau of Investigation
FBI OVA – Federal Bureau of Investigation, Office for Victim Assistance
NIJ – Office of Justice Programs, National Institute of Justice
OJJDP – Office of Justice Programs, Office of Juvenile Justice and Delinquency Prevention
OJP – Office of Justice Programs
OVC – Office of Justice Programs, Office for Victims of Crime
OVW – Office on Violence Against Women
USAO – United States Attorneys' Offices

Department of Health and Human Services (HHS) Entities

ACF – Administration for Children and Families
CDC – Centers for Disease Control and Prevention
HRSA – Health Resources and Services Administration
ORR – Office of Refugee Resettlement
SAMHSA – Substance Abuse and Mental Health Services Administration

Department of Homeland Security (DHS) Entities

CBP – U.S. Customs and Border Protection
CFBNP – Center for Faith-based and Neighborhood Partnerships
FEMA – Federal Emergency Management Agency
FLETC – Federal Law Enforcement Training Centers
HSI VAP – U.S. Immigration and Customs Enforcement, Homeland Security Investigations, Victim Assistance Program
ICE – U.S. Immigration and Customs Enforcement
ICE HSI – U.S. Immigration and Customs Enforcement, Homeland Security Investigations
OHA – Office of Health Affairs
USCG – U.S. Coast Guard
USCIS – U.S. Citizenship and Immigration Services

Other Government Offices and Entities

DOD – Department of Defense
DOL – Department of Labor
DOS – Department of State
DOS DS – Department of State, Bureau of Diplomatic Security
DOS TIP Office – Department of State, Office to Monitor and Combat Trafficking in Persons
DOT – Department of Transportation
ED – Department of Education
EEOC – Equal Employment Opportunity Commission
HSTC – Human Smuggling and Trafficking Center
HUD – Department of Housing and Urban Development
PITF – President's Interagency Task Force to Monitor and Combat Trafficking in Persons
SPOG – Senior Policy Operating Group
USAID – U.S. Agency for International Development

Other Acronyms

AI/AN – American Indian/Alaska Native
CSEC – Commercial Sexual Exploitation of Children
LGBTQ - Lesbian, Gay, Bisexual, Transgender, and Questioning
NCMEC – National Center for Missing and Exploited Children
TVPA – Trafficking Victims Protection Act
VAWA – Violence Against Women Act
VOCA – Victims of Crime Act

APPENDIX B: TIMELINE

OVERARCHING THEMES: INTEGRATE SURVIVOR EXPERIENCES AND INPUT

AGENCY	ACTION	FY13	FY14	FY15	FY16	FY17	BEYOND
OVC with DHS, DOS TIP Office, ACF, EOUSA, and COPS	Host a forum to hear from survivors of trafficking about effective, strategic, and meaningful ways to engage survivor groups		X				
DHS	Engage nongovernmental stakeholders, including survivors, in meetings twice a year	X	X	X	X	X	X
ACF, HSI VAP, FBI, and OVC	Integrate survivor experiences and perspectives into training and technical assistance materials	X	X	X	X	X	X
EOUSA	Distribute guidance to the USAO task forces encouraging survivor input where appropriate		X				
ACF	Explore the creation of a public platform to receive ongoing feedback on the quality of services, including gaps in service and challenges to service delivery		X				

OVERARCHING THEMES: STANDARDS OF CARE

AGENCY	ACTION	FY13	FY14	FY15	FY16	FY17	BEYOND
OVC	Publish *Achieving Excellence: Model Standards for Serving Victims and Survivors of Crime*, which includes program, competency, and ethical standards for crime victim service providers		X				
ACF with DHS and DOJ	Identify minimum standards of care required by grant recipients			X			

OBJECTIVE 1: PROVIDE FEDERAL LEADERSHIP AND DIRECTION TO IMPROVE VICTIM SERVICES.

AGENCY	ACTION	FY13	FY14	FY15	FY16	FY17	BEYOND
IMPLEMENT RECOMMENDATIONS FOR SYSTEMIC CHANGE							
OJJDP with ACF, SAMSA, CDC, DOI, CNCS, USDA, OVC, and OVW	Implement the recommendations in *Defending Childhood*	X	X	X	X	X	X
OJJDP	Conduct public hearings and listening sessions to help the Task Force on American Indian/ Alaska Native Children Exposed to Violence gain understanding of AI/AN children's exposure to human trafficking		X				
OVC	Publish Vision 21: *Transforming Victim Services*	X					
DHS, DOS TIP Office, HHS, and USAID	Implement recommendations in the *President's Advisory Council on Faith-based and Neighborhood Partnerships Report*		X				
ACF	Rollout guidance on child trafficking for child welfare and runaway and homeless youth systems	X					
IDENTIFY PROMISING PRACTICES							
DHS, DOJ, DOS TIP Office, ED, and HHS	Explore convening meetings where allied professionals share lessons learned to inform the development of federal anti-human trafficking efforts			X			
OVW with ACF	Gather stakeholder's input on the role of domestic violence and sexual assault providers in addressing human trafficking and any promising practices		X				
NIJ	Release an evaluation of the FY 2009 OVC Services to *Domestic Minor Victims of Human Trafficking* grants		X				
OVC	Publish a survivor-created guide on developing culturally competent services for commercially sexually exploited and trafficked girls and young women		X				
ACF	Assess and disseminate analysis of pilot programs on human trafficking within the runaway and homeless youth program			X			
ACF and SAMHSA	Provide recommendations on the mental health needs of victims based on the Assistant Secretary for Planning and Evaluation's 2008 National Symposium on the Health Needs of Human Trafficking Victims		X				

OBJECTIVE 2: COORDINATE VICTIM SERVICES EFFECTIVELY THROUGH COLLABORATION ACROSS MULTIPLE SERVICE SECTORS.

AGENCY	ACTION	FY13	FY14	FY15	FY16	FY17	BEYOND
DEVELOP AND PROMOTE STANDARD TERMINOLOGY							
OVC with DHS, DOL, DOS TIP Office, EEOC, ACF, and COPS	Update, translate, print, and disseminate *Trafficking in Persons: A Guide for Non-Governmental Organizations* with common terminology for federal agencies			X			
ACF	Clarify and provide guidance on the definitions of child sex trafficking and commercial sexual exploitation of children		X				
COPS	Update human trafficking-related publications to include consistent language		X	X	X		
ENSURE FEDERAL FUNDING IS STRATEGICALLY COORDINATED							
ACF	Explore effective funding models for victim services	X					
OVC, OVW, and ACF	Review guidance and solicitation language to coordinate federal funding and expand partnerships	X	X	X	X	X	X
OVC, BJA, and ACF	Consider ways to coordinate grant performance measurements and data collection methods		X	X			
OVC and BJA	Publish solicitations and award grants for Anti-Human Trafficking Task Forces	X	X	X	X	X	X
OVW	Include human trafficking in VAWA grant solicitations where allowable and appropriate			X			
OVW	Train staff and grantees on providing VAWA- funded services to trafficking victims	X					
COPS	Consider incorporating human trafficking training in Community Policing Development solicitation		X				
OJJDP	Continue program planning that considers support of human trafficking efforts	X	X	X	X	X	X

AGENCY	ACTION	FY13	FY14	FY15	FY16	FY17	BEYOND
	IMPROVE COORDINATION AT THE NATIONAL, REGIONAL, STATE, TERRITORIAL, TRIBAL, AND LOCAL LEVELS
Relevant federal agencies	Identify regional and local offices and points of contact for human trafficking		X	X	X		
DHS, DOJ, HHS	Coordinate implementation of Plan, identify opportunities for enhanced coordination, and share Plan reports	X	X	X	X	X	
DOJ	Meet quarterly to discuss and coordinate intra-agency activities	X	X	X	X	X	X
HHS	Meet quarterly to discuss and coordinate intra-agency activities	X	X	X	X	X	X
ACF	Explore coordinating with the AmeriCorps VISTA program	X					
ACF	Draft a 3-year plan for innovative outreach programming	X					
DHS Blue Campaign Steering Committee	Define and prioritize cross-cutting strategic projects for intra-agency human trafficking-related capabilities	X	X	X	X	X	X
DOS	Address A-3 and G-5 workers through regular internal working group meetings	X	X	X	X	X	X
DOS	Annually brief stakeholders about efforts to protect and identify victims	X	X	X	X	X	X

OBJECTIVE 3: ESTABLISH BASELINE KNOWLEDGE OF HUMAN TRAFFICKING AND VICTIM SERVICE NEEDS THROUGH RIGOROUS RESEARCH AND REPORTING.

AGENCY	ACTION	FY13	FY14	FY15	FY16	FY17	BEYOND
RESEARCH HUMAN TRAFFICKING IN THE UNITED STATES							
SPOG Research and Data Committee	Share information on U.S. Government-funded human trafficking research projects	X	X	X	X	X	X
NIJ	Release two studies on labor trafficking in the United States	X	X				
NIJ	Complete a study on the United States' unlawful commercial sex economy		X				
NIJ	Release a study of the effectiveness of interventions with foreign national human trafficking victims		X				
NIJ	Release a study that assesses the effectiveness of state human trafficking legislation		X				
NIJ	Conclude a study on the underreporting of trafficked minors in Illinois				X		
ACF	Examine the results of a 2-year pre-employment services pilot program for human trafficking victims		X				
OJJDP	Complete a study on the prevalence of CSEC, including sex trafficking, in the United States			X			
OJJDP	Release a study on CSEC in the United States, including recommended strategies	X					
OJJDP	Assess the characteristics and needs of LGBTQ and young men who have sex with men populations involved in commercial sex			X			
OVW with NIJ	Study the impact of the population boom in western North Dakota and eastern Montana on domestic violence, dating violence, sexual assault, stalking, and human trafficking				X		
IDENTIFY RESOURCE GAPS							
OVC with BJA and HSTC	Provide federal agencies with GIS mapping of services and collaborations and investigations to identify gaps		X	X	X	X	X
OJJDP and OVC	Conduct informal assessment of grant-funded Task Forces		X				
OVC, OVW, and ACF	Gather information on the needs of trafficked AI/AN women and girls and promising practices for service delivery		X				

AGENCY	ACTION	FY13	FY14	FY15	FY16	FY17	BEYOND
OVC, OVW, and ACF	Gather information on the needs of trafficked boys and men, LGBTQ victims, and minor victims of labor trafficking	X	X	X	X	X	X
OVW	Explore providing funds to law enforcement and victim service providers in western North Dakota and eastern Montana	X	X				
ESTABLISH NEW DATA COLLECTION MECHANISMS							
FBI	Build a data collection application for all civil rights investigations to include human trafficking cases		X				
OJJDP	Assist Internet Crimes Against Children Task Forces to report data on trafficking cases	X	X	X	X	X	X
OVW	Include human trafficking in grantee and subgrantee report forms and in Congressional reporting			X			
OVC	Revise draft grantee and subgrantee data collection forms for VOCA Assistance and Compensation Programs to include human trafficking, where appropriate			X			
NIJ	Host an expert working group to tackle barriers hampering data collection and research on human trafficking		X				
HSTC	Convene an interagency working group to explore sustaining data gathering and analysis		X				
EEOC	Explore ways of tracking data on human trafficking in its internal data collection systems			X			
ACF	Explore ways to better collect data to uncover specific risk factors among children who experienced abuse or neglect and runaway and homeless youth						X
ACF	Explore possibilities for coordinating data collection on human trafficking across agency programs		X				
HHS	Explore strategies for compiling estimates on the prevalence of human trafficking in the United States		X				
HRSA	Consider adopting action from the HHS Action Plan to Reduce Racial and Ethnic Health Disparities to establish data standards related to victims of human trafficking			X			
SHARE DATA AND REPORTS							
HSTC	Share a Human Trafficking National Assessment with relevant federal agencies to identify hotspots, trends, and patterns in victim recruitment and exploitation in the United States		X				

continued on next page

continued from previous page

OBJECTIVE 3: ESTABLISH BASELINE KNOWLEDGE OF HUMAN TRAFFICKING AND VICTIM SERVICE NEEDS THROUGH RIGOROUS RESEARCH AND REPORTING.

AGENCY	ACTION	FY13	FY14	FY15	FY16	FY17	BEYOND
HSTC	Share lessons learned and best practices of data collection and compilation from the process of creating the Human Trafficking National Assessment		X				
HSTC	Make structured and cleansed data sets available to relevant federal agencies		X				
OVC	Create and disseminate annual aggregate data report		X	X	X	X	X
DOL	Collect and share publicly available labor enforcement data regarding labor exploitation	X	X	X	X	X	X
USCIS and HSI VAP	Consolidate data on victims of human trafficking and immigration benefits and publish on DHS Blue Campaign Web site		X	X	X	X	X
ACF	Release a report analyzing anti-human trafficking grantee data		X				
ACF	Disseminate analysis of human trafficking trends		X				

OBJECTIVE 4: SUPPORT THE DEVELOPMENT OF EFFECTIVE RESPONSES TO THE NEEDS OF HUMAN TRAFFICKING VICTIMS.

AGENCY	ACTION	FY13	FY14	FY15	FY16	FY17	BEYOND
EVALUATE SCREENING AND TRAINING TOOLS							
NIJ and OVC	Publish a validated screening tool and user guide for use by all trafficking assistance grantees and the field		X				
HHS	Identify targeted screening tools for various systems		X				
ACF	Explore the development of standardized health care protocols						X
IMPROVE THE QUALITY OF EVALUATIONS							
OVC and ACF	Identify common, effective performance measures for victim service outcomes			X			
OVC and ACF with NIJ	Explore ways to develop technical assistance guides, tools, and templates for evaluation				X	X	
ACF	Explore ways to evaluate effectiveness of training curricula for child welfare and runaway and homeless youth systems						X
DOD	Gauge effectiveness of human trafficking training through the Status of Forces Survey	X					

OBJECTIVE 5: INCREASE VICTIM IDENTIFICATION THROUGH COORDINATED PUBLIC OUTREACH AND AWARENESS EFFORTS.

AGENCY	ACTION	FY13	FY14	FY15	FY16	FY17	BEYOND
CONDUCT OUTREACH AND AWARENESS ACTIVITIES AND PROVIDE RESOURCES FOR THE GENERAL PUBLIC							
OVC	Create PSA to raise visibility of human trafficking		X				
DHS	Continue to hold bi-annual stakeholder engagement event	X	X	X	X	X	X
FBI OVA	Coordinate and participate in community awareness events across the country	X	X	X	X	X	X
COPS	Engage in special public outreach activities to promote federal agency guidance and identified promising practices	X	X	X	X	X	X
ACF	Strengthen engagement and awareness of human trafficking among youth		X	X			
DHS	Create a public service announcement raising awareness of human trafficking	X					
DHS	Distribute new human trafficking awareness materials for the general public and groups likely to encounter victims	X	X	X	X	X	X
DHS and DOS TIP Office	Distribute awareness-raising materials to foreign embassies and consulates in the United States	X	X	X	X	X	X
DHS, HHS, and OVC	Develop and disseminate materials for national civic organizations			X	X	X	X
DHS, HHS, and OVC	Develop and disseminate materials for national service organizations				X	X	X
DOL and EEOC with ACF	Develop and disseminate materials in relevant languages about employment rights and civil remedies		X				
ICE HSI	Distribute human trafficking awareness materials in multiple languages	X	X	X	X	X	X
USCIS	Develop and distribute human trafficking materials related to immigration benefits	X	X	X	X	X	X
FBI	Distribute human trafficking materials in multiple languages	X	X	X	X	X	X
EOUSA	Develop public awareness and outreach materials, including labor and sex trafficking toolkits		X				
DOS TIP Office	Designate victim identification as the theme of the 2013 Trafficking in Persons Report	X					
FBI Violent Crimes Against Children Section	Disseminate national billboard, bus board, and bus stop ads addressing child sexual exploitation	X	X	X	X	X	X

continued on next page

continued from previous page

OBJECTIVE 5: INCREASE VICTIM IDENTIFICATION THROUGH COORDINATED PUBLIC OUTREACH AND AWARENESS EFFORTS.

AGENCY	ACTION	FY13	FY14	FY15	FY16	FY17	BEYOND
DOS TIP Office	Raise awareness and increase demand for responsibly sourced goods and services and measure impact through the Slavery Footprint platform	X	X	X	X	X	X
DHS, DOJ, DOS TIP Office, and HHS	Expand human trafficking awareness efforts on social media	X	X	X	X	X	X
EEOC	Update Web site and social media feeds with human trafficking updates and resources		X	X	X		
CONDUCT OUTREACH AND AWARENESS ACTIVITIES AND PROVIDE RESOURCES FOR TARGETED GROUPS/COMMUNITIES							
DOL	Disseminate online toolkit for responsible businesses to reduce child and forced labor in their supply chains	X	X				
DOL	Share information to raise awareness of trafficking among National Farmworker Jobs Program grantees		X				
DOS Bureau of Consular Affairs with USCIS	Develop informational video on protections for certain visa holders for display in consular waiting rooms		X	X	X	X	X
DOS	Educate foreign mission personnel and their domestic workers about protections for domestic workers employed by diplomatic personnel	X	X	X	X	X	X
DOS	Develop procedures for the in-person registration of domestic workers employed by diplomatic personnel in the Washington, D.C., area		X	X	X	X	X
ACF	Engage with businesses to post information on the National Human Trafficking Resource Center's Web site and to discuss possibilities for meeting survivor workforce development needs			X			
HUD	Provide outreach and awareness materials to public housing agencies and Continuums of Care		X				
HHS	Develop and disseminate materials for public health organizations			X			
OJP	Support a philanthropic community forum on human trafficking				X		
DHS and DOT	Release the Blue Lightning Initiative, work to expand Blue Lightning to foreign-based airlines and personnel	X	X	X			

AGENCY	ACTION	FY13	FY14	FY15	FY16	FY17	BEYOND
DHS and DOT	Train all Amtrak employees and Amtrak police department officers to identify and report suspected cases of human trafficking	X	X	X	X	X	X
DOT	Work with Transportation Leaders Against Human Trafficking to encourage corporate participation, employee training, and public outreach campaigns across the transportation industry	X	X	X			
DHS, OJJDP, ED, and ACF	Develop and disseminate materials for youth		X	X	X	X	X
DOL with ACF	Share information to raise awareness of trafficking among YouthBuild grantees		X				
USAID	Disseminate findings of the Campus Challenge Research grants			X			

OBJECTIVE 6: BUILD CAPACITY TO BETTER IDENTIFY AND SERVE VICTIMS THROUGH TARGETED TRAINING AND TECHNICAL ASSISTANCE.

AGENCY	ACTION	FY13	FY14	FY15	FY16	FY17	BEYOND
EXPAND TRAINING OF FEDERAL GOVERNMENT EMPLOYEES							
USDA	Make human trafficking training available to all personnel		X				
DOD	Update law enforcement training	X					
DOD	Update general human trafficking awareness training and create refresher course, require contractors to prove awareness	X					
DOD	Educate troops through targeted media efforts	X	X	X	X	X	X
DOD	Distribute human trafficking awareness materials	X	X	X	X	X	X
HHS	Provide guidance for increased partnerships with HHS regional offices	X					
HHS	Determine appropriate personnel, grantees, and subcontractors for training on human trafficking, develop content and standards, and integrate the training as a standard requirement	X	X	X	X	X	X
ICE	Provide mandatory training for all ICE personnel likely to encounter victims of human trafficking	X	X	X	X	X	X
ICE HSI	Provide periodic training to HSI human trafficking subject matter experts	X	X	X	X	X	X

continued on next page

continued from previous page

OBJECTIVE 6: BUILD CAPACITY TO BETTER IDENTIFY AND SERVE VICTIMS THROUGH TARGETED TRAINING AND TECHNICAL ASSISTANCE.

AGENCY	ACTION	FY13	FY14	FY15	FY16	FY17	BEYOND
ICE HSI	Conduct 2-week advanced human smuggling and trafficking courses at FLETC	X	X	X	X	X	X
USCIS	Provide mandatory human trafficking training to public-facing employees	X	X	X	X	X	X
USCIS	Provide periodic training on human trafficking and immigration benefits to USCIS community relations officers	X	X	X	X	X	X
USCIS	Provide training to all new officers at the USCIS Refugee, Asylum, and International Operations Directorate	X	X	X	X	X	X
USCG	Maintain online DHS Blue Campaign human trafficking training on USCG training portal for all USCG personnel	X	X	X	X	X	X
CBP	Provide annual training to officers and agents on human trafficking	X	X	X	X	X	X
FEMA	Provide general human trafficking awareness training to field-deployable employees	X	X	X	X	X	X
DHS Office of Health Affairs and FEMA	Support outreach and training efforts to engage DHS medical first responder personnel	X	X	X	X	X	X
DHS Office of Health Affairs with HHS	Support outreach and training efforts to engage medical first responder personnel and hospital staff	X	X	X	X	X	X
DHS and DOJ	Coordinate cross training between federal law enforcement victim assistance specialists with federally funded service providers	X	X	X	X	X	X
FBI	Train agents and victim specialists working in Indian Country on all aspects of human trafficking		X				
FBI	Develop human trafficking awareness training for all FBI employees			X			
FBI	Provide human trafficking training to supervisors, agents, intelligence analysts, and victim specialists assigned work on human trafficking	X	X	X	X	X	X
FBI Violent Crimes Against Children Section	Provide training regarding the protection of victims and utilization of FBI Task Force resources in child sex trafficking investigations	X	X	X	X	X	X
FBI	Provide training to all investigative personnel and victim specialists on supporting Continued Presence and T visa applications	X	X	X	X	X	X

AGENCY	ACTION	FY13	FY14	FY15	FY16	FY17	BEYOND
FBI	Provide human trafficking training to additional DOJ entities		X				
EOUSA	Provide training on human trafficking resources, victim identification, and cultural sensitivity for victim-witness personnel		X				
DOL	Make general awareness training available to all personnel	X	X				
DOL	Finalize basic awareness and referral training for all Wage and Hour Division investigators and make it available to Occupational Safety and Health Administration regional management and state counterparts	X	X				
DOL	Determine appropriate sub-agencies for human trafficking training and develop training content and standards	X	X				
DOS	Make human trafficking training available to all personnel		X				
DOS Foreign Service Institute	Educate consular officers about the overseas adjudication of T and U visas and the *Know Your Rights* pamphlet	X	X	X	X	X	X
DOS Foreign Service Institute	Train mid-level officers on T and U visas	X	X	X	X	X	X
DOS Visa Office	Train the DOS Public Inquiries Division on human trafficking	X	X	X	X	X	X
DOS DS	Create an online human trafficking education course that includes information on how to identify victims, best practices for investigation and prosecution, and referral for services		X	X	X	X	X
DOT	Train employees on general human trafficking awareness	X	X	X	X	X	X
EEOC	Determine appropriate personnel for training on human trafficking and develop content and standards		X	X	X		
EEOC	Work with State Fair Employment Practices Agencies to provide updates and training on labor trafficking			X	X		
USAID	Train all personnel on the Agency's Counter-Trafficking in Persons Code of Conduct; conduct due diligence prior to awarding contracts, grants, and cooperative agreements; and respond to allegations of abuse	X	X	X	X	X	X

continued on next page

continued from previous page

OBJECTIVE 6: BUILD CAPACITY TO BETTER IDENTIFY AND SERVE VICTIMS THROUGH TARGETED TRAINING AND TECHNICAL ASSISTANCE.

AGENCY	ACTION	FY13	FY14	FY15	FY16	FY17	BEYOND
TRAIN AND ASSIST STATE, TERRITORIAL, TRIBAL, AND LOCAL LAW ENFORCEMENT AND CRIMINAL JUSTICE SYSTEMS							
DHS and DOJ, with DOL	Develop common teaching points on victim-centered approaches to investigation for law enforcement trainings			X			
ICE HSI, FLETC, USCIS, BJA, FBI, OJJDP, OVC, and OVW	Provide training and technical assistance resources, including roll call videos, training materials, and speakers to national law enforcement membership organizations	X	X	X	X	X	X
ICE HSI and FLETC	Produce and distribute two roll call videos for state and local law enforcement that explain how immigration benefits can benefit investigations					X	
ICE HSI and FLETC	Expand the reach of its state and local law enforcement Web-based human trafficking awareness training	X	X	X	X	X	X
DHS with SPOG, DOL, and EEOC	Include information on labor trafficking and exploitation in the FLETC law enforcement training		X	X			
ICE HSI and USCIS	Revise and deliver training to federal, state, territorial, tribal, and local law enforcement	X	X	X	X	X	X
USCIS	Produce a T visa resource guide for law enforcement and provide U visa resource guide		X				
DHS OHA, FEMA, ICE HSI, and FLETC	Provide general awareness training for first responder communities	X	X	X	X	X	X
DHS	Distribute human trafficking awareness video and indicator cards for first responders	X	X	X	X	X	X
DOT	Train state and local law enforcement to detect human trafficking on trucks and buses	X	X	X	X	X	X
COPS	Develop a *Commercial Sexual Exploitation of Children Toolkit for Law Enforcement*		X				
FBI	Conduct investigative trainings for law enforcement personnel	X	X	X	X	X	X
DHS, DOJ, and DOL	Provide advanced human trafficking training for each Anti-Trafficking Coordination Team	X	X	X			
OVC	Update and enhance the *Anti-Human Trafficking Task Force Strategy and Operations e-Guide*, including strategies for outreach and awareness		X				

AGENCY	ACTION	FY13	FY14	FY15	FY16	FY17	BEYOND
FBI Civil Rights Unit and Violent Crimes Against Children Section	Coordinate with the FBI's intelligence fusion cells to assess, rank, and address human trafficking threats and locate victims	X	X	X	X	X	X
BJA	Design and deliver a human trafficking training for tribal law enforcement	X	X				
DHS, OJJDP, and ACF	Provide training materials about trafficking of children to juvenile justice system stakeholders		X				
State Justice Institute	Support the *Human Trafficking and the State Courts Collaborative* to increase state courts' awareness of human trafficking	X	X				
OJJDP with HSI VAP, ACF, and NCMEC	Develop and deliver a curriculum on how to conduct forensic interviews with child victims of commercial sexual exploitation	X	X	X	X	X	X
HSI VAP	Explore the feasibility of increasing the number of forensic interviewers as funding allows	X					
BJA	Explore opportunities to continue to provide curriculum for state prosecutors on human trafficking	X	X				
BJA with OVC	Explore options to provide funding to train law enforcement, prosecutors, and state judges on appropriate responses to victims	X	X	X	X	X	X
TRAIN AND ASSIST SERVICE PROVIDERS WORKING WITH VICTIMS OF HUMAN TRAFFICKING							
FBI, OVC, DOL, and ACF	Provide training and technical assistance to anti-human trafficking organizations on developing relationships with business, labor, and philanthropic leaders	X	X				
OVC and BJA, with ACF	Host a Regional Task Force Training Forum		X				
DOS DS	Educate the nongovernmental organization community about ability of DOS DS to identify human trafficking victims and work on cases	X	X	X	X	X	X
HSI VAP, OVC, OVW, ACF, and SAMHSA	Develop and provide training on the impact of trauma and polyvictimization on victims and the need for trauma-informed care		X	X	X	X	X
OJJDP and ACF	Offer training on gender-specific services to providers working with child victims		X				

continued on next page

continued from previous page

OBJECTIVE 6: BUILD CAPACITY TO BETTER IDENTIFY AND SERVE VICTIMS THROUGH TARGETED TRAINING AND TECHNICAL ASSISTANCE.

AGENCY	ACTION	FY13	FY14	FY15	FY16	FY17	BEYOND
OJJDP	Provide training and technical assistance to state, territorial, tribal, and local partners who recover child abduction victims	X	X	X	X	X	X
HSI VAP and USCIS	Conduct trainings on combating human trafficking and immigration benefit options for victims	X	X	X	X	X	X
ACF with DOJ and DHS	Provide guidance on safe and ethical victim outreach practices	X					
OVC	Produce a new human trafficking training video			X			
OVC	Provide anti-human trafficking grantees with access to training on trauma-informed care practices	X	X	X	X	X	X
OVC	Provide anti-human trafficking grantees with training on supporting victims of human trafficking in accessing services needed to attain stability and independence	X	X	X	X	X	X
TRAIN AND ASSIST THE BROADER VICTIM SERVICES FIELD							
HHS	Provide training resources to refugee resettlement, child welfare, runaway and homeless youth, domestic violence, and tribal community grantees		X				
OVC	Provide targeted training and technical assistance for VOCA administrators	X	X	X	X	X	X
OVC	Review Victim Assistance Training Online and the National Victim Assistance Academy curricula and add information on human trafficking	X					
OVC	Support a human trafficking training at the National Symposium on Child Abuse		X				
OVC	Modify the *Supporting Crime Victims with Disabilities* instructor-led training and *Promising Practices to Serving Victims with Disabilities Toolkit* to include human trafficking and make available to practitioners in contact with persons with disabilities who are at risk of being trafficked	X	X	X	X	X	X
OVC	Include specific content and resources on trafficking of persons with disabilities in the *Anti-Human Trafficking Task Force Strategy and Operations e-Guide*	X	X				
FBI	Provide trainings with and to victims service providers, community leaders, faith-based, and other nongovernmental organizations	X	X	X	X	X	X

AGENCY	ACTION	FY13	FY14	FY15	FY16	FY17	BEYOND
FLETC	Enhance and expand training and technical assistance to entities seeking to create training on human trafficking identification and victim assistance	X	X	X	X	X	X
ICE HSI and USCIS	Revise and deliver training to victim service providers and immigration attorneys	X	X	X	X	X	X
ACF Family and Youth Services Bureau	Provide training for Family Violence Prevention and Services Act Program State Administrators, tribal grantees, and state domestic violence coalitions	X					
ACF, OVC, and OVW	Provide annual training and technical assistance on intersections of human trafficking, domestic violence, and sexual assault	X	X	X	X	X	X
ACF	Offer at least one webinar for domestic violence victim service providers based on the Asian Pacific Islander Institute on Domestic Violence's *Considerations and Recommendations for Battered Women's Advocates*	X					
OVW	Expand collaboration at the local level between OVW and stakeholders in the domestic violence, sexual assault, and anti-human trafficking fields through multidisciplinary training					X	
OVW	Provide at least one webinar for grantees on how to identify and respond to minor sex trafficking and build collaborations					X	
TRAIN AND ASSIST ALLIED PROFESSIONALS							
ED	Develop a guide for school personnel on child sex trafficking and continue to partner with school districts to reduce human trafficking on campuses	X	X				
DHS, ED, and ACF	Develop and disseminate training materials and resources	X	X				
ED and DHS	Disseminate products co-branded with the Blue Campaign for use in and by schools		X				
ACF	Explore partnering with social work schools, counseling schools, and related professional associations to increase training for health professionals	X					
ACF	Explore training opportunities for family service workers in Head Start programs		X				
ACF and HRSA	Consider strategies to raise awareness about human trafficking in community colleges			X			

continued on next page

continued from previous page

OBJECTIVE 6: BUILD CAPACITY TO BETTER IDENTIFY AND SERVE VICTIMS THROUGH TARGETED TRAINING AND TECHNICAL ASSISTANCE.

AGENCY	ACTION	FY13	FY14	FY15	FY16	FY17	BEYOND
CFBNP and HSI VAP	Conduct and evaluate a pilot training and technical assistance initiative for faith-based and other community-based organizations	X					
CFBNP, HSI VAP with OVC, DOL, ACF, and HUD	Provide training and technical assistance to two faith-based and other community-based organizations per year, and disseminate materials and strategies		X	X	X	X	X
DOL with DOJ and HHS	Provide updated training on trafficking issues to the State Farmworker Monitor Advocates	X	X				
DOL	Deliver two webinar trainings to the workforce investment system, highlighting promising practices in employment and training services	X	X				
HHS	Educate the health care community about human trafficking to increase services and support for victims			X			
HHS	Provide guidance on addressing major gaps in medical treatment and services for victims of human trafficking		X				
ACF	Form technical working group of health care professionals to increase training and collaboration for health care professionals on meeting the needs of human trafficking victims	X					

OBJECTIVE 7: FOSTER COLLABORATIONS AND PARTNERSHIPS TO ENHANCE THE COMMUNITY RESPONSE TO HUMAN TRAFFICKING.

AGENCY	ACTION	FY13	FY14	FY15	FY16	FY17	BEYOND
HHS	Work with medical, educational, and other stakeholder communities to identify human trafficking of service-related professionals, including elder care providers and teachers		X				
HHS	Reach out to community partners who can aid in victim identification, including health care providers, unions, and housing authorities and inspectors			X			
DOD	Make trainings more victim-centered and ensure troops know where to refer victims for assistance		X				
FBI	Coordinate anti-trafficking efforts through partnerships with hotels, medical facilities, and through trainings at Citizens Academies	X	X	X	X	X	X

OBJECTIVE 7: FOSTER COLLABORATIONS AND PARTNERSHIPS TO ENHANCE THE COMMUNITY RESPONSE TO HUMAN TRAFFICKING.

AGENCY	ACTION	FY13	FY14	FY15	FY16	FY17	BEYOND
FBI	Foster greater relationships with juvenile detention facility personnel		X				
FBI OVA	Establish public-private partnerships through victim specialist outreach		X				
EOUSA	Partner with nonprofit organizations and other agencies through USAO task forces	X	X	X	X	X	X
ICE HSI	Develop partnerships	X	X	X	X	X	X
DHS	Pursue co-branding partnerships with Blue Campaign training materials	X	X	X	X	X	X
EEOC	Work on targeted outreach and expansion of partnerships to protect victims' rights	X	X	X	X	X	X
FBI	Broaden community outreach efforts within AI/AN communities		X				
HHS	Incorporate human trafficking in tribal consultations and identify distribution channels to relevant programs through HHS's Indian Health Service	X	X	X	X	X	X
DHS OHA	Coordinate tribal outreach through tribal emergency medicine associations	X	X	X	X	X	X
EOUSA	Form partnerships between USAO task forces and faith-based and community-based organizations	X	X	X	X	X	X
HSI VAP and FBI	Participate on human trafficking and FBI Child Exploitation Task Forces to develop partnerships with faith-based, cultural, ethnic, and other community-based organizations	X	X	X	X	X	X
DOL, EEOC, and HHS	Leverage relationships with domestic worker, farmworker, guest worker, worker centers, workers' advocacy organizations, and other labor organizations to identify opportunities for victim identification and connection to services		X				
ACF	Work with runaway and homeless youth programs to identify opportunities for victim identification in exploitative peddling operations		X				
ED	Work with the National Center for Homeless Education to make anti-human trafficking resources available	X	X				

continued on next page

continued from previous page

OBJECTIVE 7: FOSTER COLLABORATIONS AND PARTNERSHIPS TO ENHANCE THE COMMUNITY RESPONSE TO HUMAN TRAFFICKING.

AGENCY	ACTION	FY13	FY14	FY15	FY16	FY17	BEYOND
DEVELOP NETWORKS TO EXPAND ACCESS TO SERVICES							
OVC, OJJDP, DOS TIP Office, ACF, and HUD	Engage in a public-private capacity-building initiative with Humanity United	X	X				
DHS, DOJ, and ACF	Coordinate efforts to use victim assistance and prosecution-based specialists to connect victims to services		X	X	X	X	X
OVC, DOL, and ACF	Strengthen an informal network around the issue of employment and training services for victims of trafficking to share information and identify promising practices	X	X	X	X	X	X
ACF	Explore possibilities to engage the Assets for Independence Program		X				
DOL and ACF	Facilitate relationships between community-based organizations and business communities and industries to support employment services and workforce development for victims		X				
OJJDP	Expand evidence-based mentoring initiatives to develop outreach to child victims and provide training to mentoring experts		X				
OVC	Provide additional guidance to anti-human trafficking grantees on provision of services to family members of victims		X				
ED	Strengthen coordination among, and provide guidance to, migrant youth, runaway and homeless youth, and other relevant programs	X	X				
ED	Develop webinar for school community grantees on identification and response to minor sex trafficking victims	X					

OBJECTIVE 8: IMPROVE ACCESS TO VICTIM SERVICES BY REMOVING SYSTEMIC BARRIERS.

AGENCY	ACTION	FY13	FY14	FY15	FY16	FY17	BEYOND
IMPROVE ACCESS TO SERVICES AND BENEFITS							
ACF	Review current policies, practices, regulations, and statutes guiding runaway and homeless youth and domestic violence shelters and consider strategies to remove barriers		X				
ACF with HUD	Review federal policy regarding homelessness and requirements that may prevent victims of human trafficking from qualifying for housing	X					
ACF	Review how policies affecting youth aging out of foster care impact victims of human trafficking and explore possibilities to recruit and train specialized foster parents		X				
ACF	Explore public-private partnerships with businesses, philanthropic foundations, faith-based and other community organizations, and leaders to support ongoing housing needs			X			
OVC with ACF, HUD, NIJ, and OVW	Evaluate the appropriateness and feasibility of housing demonstration projects					X	
HSI VAP, FBI OVA, and USAO	Make referrals to local service provider organizations to provide appropriate housing for victims in federal investigations and prosecutions	X	X	X	X	X	X
OVC	Engage in *Legal Assistance for Crime Victims: An OVC Capacity Building Initiative* to build capacity for legal services for all crime victims, including victims of human trafficking	X	X	X	X	X	X
OVC	Explore ways to support and strengthen Wraparound Victim Legal Assistance Network Demonstration Projects to provide comprehensive legal services to crime victims						X
OVC, OVW, and ACF, with DOJ Access to Justice Initiative	Explore opportunities to partner with legal service providers to provide training on identifying human trafficking victims and provision of comprehensive legal services	X	X	X	X	X	X
OVC, OVW, and ACF	Provide grant funding to support legal services, and develop and provide training and technical assistance	X	X	X	X	X	X
HSI VAP, FBI OVA, and USAO	Make referrals to appropriate legal service providers for victims of human trafficking in federal investigations and prosecutions	X	X	X	X	X	X
DHS	Update T nonimmigrant status regulations to provide clearer guidance	X					
ICE HSI, FBI OVA, and USAO	Assist in the coordination of Continued Presence, law enforcement certifications for the T and U visa and referrals to immigration attorneys	X	X	X	X	X	X

continued on next page

continued from previous page

OBJECTIVE 8: IMPROVE ACCESS TO VICTIM SERVICES BY REMOVING SYSTEMIC BARRIERS.

AGENCY	ACTION	FY13	FY14	FY15	FY16	FY17	BEYOND
USCIS and ICE HSI	Train law enforcement and immigration attorneys on Continued Presence and T and U visas	X	X	X	X	X	X
USCIS	Provide training to adjudicators of the T and U visas at the Vermont Service Center	X	X	X	X	X	X
USCIS	Provide information and resources to USCIS Fraud Detection and National Security units about suspect companies, employers, and recruiters identified during the adjudication of T visas	X	X	X	X	X	X
ICE HSI and USCIS	Issue Continued Presence, provide referrals to HHS, and issue employment authorization documents	X	X	X	X	X	X
DOL with USCIS	Explore feasibility of completing law enforcement declarations for T visas		X	X			
EEOC with USCIS	Examine feasibility of providing certifications for T visas		X	X			
OVC	Work to increase access to crime victims compensation for human trafficking victims through policy clarification, information, training, and technical assistance to state VOCA compensation program administrators		X	X	X	X	X
INCREASE ACCESS FOR VULNERABLE POPULATIONS							
ACF	Provide a directory of language access options available through service providers, and identify innovative uses of technology		X				
DHS	Provide language identification and access tools	X	X	X	X	X	X
DHS	Translate Blue Campaign awareness products into various languages		X				
EEOC	Ensure that language access officers and other employees are familiar with current trends and signs of human trafficking		X	X			
USAO	Ensure that human trafficking victims with limited English proficiency can participate meaningfully in federal prosecutions	X	X	X	X	X	X
HHS	Promote policies, training, and outreach efforts to ensure victims with disabilities receive necessary auxiliary aids and services			X			
ACF	Explore public-private partnerships to support the needs of victims with disabilities			X			
ICE HSI	Support forensic interviewers for victims of all ages and special populations, including victims with disabilities	X					
DHS	Ensure full inclusion and equal access for all persons with disabilities who interact with DHS, including victims of trafficking	X	X	X	X	X	X
FBI OVA	Provide training to FBI personnel on working with human trafficking victims with disabilities		X				
EEOC	Consider development of outreach and training materials to address issues involving trafficking of individuals with disabilities			X	X		

APPENDIX C:
PUBLIC COMMENT SUBMISSIONS

A draft version of this Federal Strategic Action Plan was released for a 45-day public comment period on April 9, 2013. During that time, the co-chair agencies received more than 337 comments online, and an additional 62 comments were sent in letters and via e-mail. In addition to comments from 127 individuals, the co-chairs received comments from the following state, local, tribal, and community organizations:

Abolition International

AEquitas

Aim Truancy Solutions

American Association of University Women

American Bar Association

American Gateways

American Medical Women's Association

API Chaya

API Legal Outreach

Aurora University

Babson Social Innovation Lab

Baltimore Child Abuse Center

Best Practices Policy Project

Businesses Ending Slavery and Trafficking

California State Senate Office of Research

Cape Counseling Services

Cape Fear Community College

Catholic Charities Fort Worth

Center for Adolescent Health & the Law

Central Council Tlingit Haida Indian Tribes of Alaska

Central Washington Comprehensive Mental Health

Chicago Alliance Against Sexual Exploitation

Children at Risk

Children of the Night

Christian Medical Association

City of Boston, Massachusetts

City of Long View, Texas

City of Waynesboro, Virginia

Civil Society

Clearimage Investigations

Coalition Against Trafficking in Women

Coalition of Immokalee Workers

Collaborative Initiative to End Human Trafficking

Columbia University

Concerned Women for America

Cook Inlet Tribal Council

County of Alameda, California

County of Bexar, Texas

County of Hennepin, Minnesota

County of McCracken, Kentucky

County of Multnomah, Oregon

County Welfare Directors Association of CA

Covenant Health Systems

Covenant House New York

Crittenton Services for Children and Families

Demand Abolition

Denver Anti-Trafficking Alliance

Devereux

ECPAT USA

Equality Now

Erotic Service Providers Legal, Education and Research Project

Florida Gulf Coast University

Free the Captives

Freedom House of Parker County

Freedom Network USA

Fresno Economic Opportunities Commission

Fulton County Department of Housing & Human Services

Georgetown University

Georgia Department of Human Services

Girls Education and Mentoring Services

Global Freedom Center

Graham Windham

H.E.A.T. Watch

Heartland Alliance

Homeless Youth Project

Human Rights Project for Girls

Human Trafficking Awareness Partnerships, Inc.

Humanity United

Hunt Alternatives Fund

I Know Better

Immigration Counseling Services

International Human Rights Clinic at Santa Clara University School of Law

International Institute of Boston

International Institute of Buffalo

International Institute of Connecticut

International Institute of New England

International Rescue Committee

International Rescue Committee Seattle

Jewish Family Services of Metropolitan Detroit

Justice Society

Kristi House

Laboratory to Combat Human Trafficking

Leadership Conference of Women Religious

League of Women Voters

Massachusetts Alliance on Teen Pregnancy

Mew Films

Michigan Crime Victim Services Commission Victim Assistant Grant Program

Michigan State University

Minnesota Indian Women's Resource Center

Mosaic Services

My Gift Program, Inc.

National Association for Children of Alcoholics

National CASA Association

National Center for Missing & Exploited Children

National Center for Victims of Crime

National Children's Alliance

National Conference of State Legislatures

National Council of Juvenile and Family Court Judges

National Council on Crime and Delinquency

National Domestic Workers Alliance

National Network for Youth

National Network to End Domestic Violence

National Survivor Network

Network of Victim Assistance

New Jersey Family Planning League

Nomi Network

North Carolina Coalition Against Sexual Assault

Northeastern University

Northern Tier Anti-Trafficking Consortium

Office of District Attorney – Denver, Colorado

Office of the Attorney General – Indiana

Office of the Attorney General – Massachusetts

Office of the Attorney General – Ohio

Ohio Department of Public Safety/Office of Criminal Justice Services

Oklahoma Coalition Against Domestic Violence & Sexual Assault

On Eagles Wings Ministries/The OEW Hope House

Opening Doors

Partners Health Care

Polaris Project

Practical Solutions to Trafficking

Renewal Forum

Resident

Resource Center for Survivors of Sexual Assault & Family Violence

Rights 4 Girls

Safe Horizon

San Diego State University

Sasha Bruce Youthworks

Sex Trafficking Survivors United

Shared Hope International

Sheridan AZ Law

Sisters of Charity of Nazareth

Sisters of Charity of New York Trafficking Task Force

Slavery Today

Southeast Technical Institute

Southern Poverty Law Center

State of Connecticut

State of Minnesota

Streetwise and Safe

Students Opposing Slavery

Task At Hand Consulting LLC

Texas Department of Family and Protective Services

The Advocates for Human Rights

The Coalition to Abolish Slavery & Trafficking

The College at Brockport

The Family Counseling Center of Fulton County

The Night Ministry

The SAGE Project

The Salvation Army National Headquarters

There is H.O.P.E. for Me, Inc.

Ujenzi Trust

University of California, Los Angeles

University of Las Vegas

University of Massachusetts, Lowell

University of Toledo

Urban Initiatives

U.S. Aftercare for Agape International Mission

U.S. Committee for Refugees and Immigrants

U.S. Conference of Catholic Bishops/Migration and Refugee Services

Vera Institute of Justice

Veronica's Voice

VIA Consulting Group

Virginia Sexual & Domestic Violence Action Alliance

Voices of Hope

Washington Engage

West Coast Children's Clinic

Western Illinois University

Women's Foundation of Minnesota

World Relief

Youth Care

Youth Spark

ENDNOTES

[1] Available at http://www.justice.gov/ag/annualreports/agreporthumantrafficking2011.pdf

[2] Pub. L. 106-386

[3] It is important to note that the federal criminal definition of labor trafficking, at 18 U.S.C. §1589 is different from this definition, which is used to define eligibility for services. In order to prove a forced labor charge, only fraud which is serious enough to compel the person to engage in the work is sufficient.

[4] 22 U.S.C. § 7102(9)-(10).

[5] *International Labour Organization 2012 Special Action Programme to Combat Forced Labour (SAP-FL)*, June 2012. http://www.ilo.org/wcmsp5/groups/public/---ed_norm/---declaration/documents/publication/wcms_182004.pdf

[6] Pub. L. 108-193

[7] Pub. L. 109-164

[8] Pub. L. 110-457

[9] *Evidence-Based Mental Health Treatment for Victims of Human Trafficking*, Erin Williamson, Nicole M. Dutch, and Heather J. Clawson; Caliber, an ICF International Company (2010).

[10] Study of HHS Programs Serving Human Trafficking Victims: Final Report (2009), available at http://aspe.hhs.gov/hsp/07/HumanTrafficking/Final/index.shtml#_Toc240256544

[11] Study of HHS Programs Serving Human Trafficking Victims: Final Report (2009), available at http://aspe.hhs.gov/hsp/07/HumanTrafficking/Final/index.shtml#_Toc240256544

[12] Study of HHS Programs Serving Human Trafficking Victims: Final Report (2009), available at http://aspe.hhs.gov/hsp/07/HumanTrafficking/Final/index.shtml#_Toc240256544

[13] Stakeholder feedback from the Victim Services Technical Working Group Meeting, December 10, 2012.

[14] Stakeholder feedback from the Victim Services Technical Working Group Meeting, December 10, 2012.

[15] Stakeholder feedback from the Victim Services Technical Working Group Meeting, December 10, 2012.

[16] Stakeholder feedback from the Victim Services Technical Working Group Meeting, December 10, 2012.

[17] Public feedback from the 45-day comment period on the Federal Strategic Action Plan on Services for Victims of Human Trafficking in the United States, June 2013.

[18] Stakeholder feedback from the Victim Services Technical Working Group Meeting, December 10, 2012.

[19] Public feedback from the 45-day comment period on the Federal Strategic Action Plan on Services for Victims of Human Trafficking in the United States, June 2013.

[20] *Addressing the Needs of Victims of Human Trafficking: Challenges, Barriers, and Promising Practices*. Heather J. Clawson and Nicole Dutch, Aug. 2008.

[21] Public feedback from the 45-day comment period on the Federal Strategic Action Plan on Services for Victims of Human Trafficking in the United States, June 2013.

[22] Stakeholder feedback from the Victim Services Technical Working Group Meeting, December 10, 2012.

[23] *2012 Trafficking in Persons Report*, U.S. Department of State.

[24] Stakeholder feedback from the Victim Services Technical Working Group Meeting, December 10, 2012.

[25] *Addressing the Needs of Victims of Human Trafficking: Challenges, Barriers, and Promising Practices*. Heather J. Clawson and Nicole Dutch, Aug. 2008.

[26] See, e.g., Crime Victims' Rights Act, 18 U.S.C. § 3771(e); Victims' Rights and Restitution Act, 42 U.S.C. §10607 (e)(2)(A); Trafficking Victims Protection Act, 22 U.S.C. § 7102(14) & (15)

[27] SAMHSA Working Definition of Trauma and Principles and Guidance for a Trauma-Informed Approach, available at http://www.samhsa.gov/traumajustice/traumadefinition/approach.aspx

[28] Public feedback from the 45-day comment period on the Federal Strategic Action Plan on Services for Victims of Human Trafficking in the United States, June 2013.

[29] Stakeholder feedback from the Victim Services Technical Working Group Meeting, December 10, 2012.

[30] Public feedback from the 45-day comment period on the Federal Strategic Action Plan on Services for Victims of Human Trafficking in the United States, June 2013.

[31] Public feedback from the 45-day comment period on the Federal Strategic Action Plan on Services for Victims of Human Trafficking in the United States, June 2013.

[32] Stakeholder feedback from the Victim Services Technical Working Group Meeting, December 10, 2012.

[33] Los Angeles Probation Department survey revealed that 59 percent of the 174 juveniles arrested on prostitution-related charges in the county were in the foster care system, and victims were often recruited by sex traffickers and pimps from group homes. Sewell, Abby. (November 27, 2012). Most of L.A. County youths held for prostitution come from foster care. *Los Angeles Times.* Available at http://articles.latimes.com/2012/nov/27/local/la-me-1128-sex-trafficking-20121128

[34] Polyvictimization refers to having experienced multiple victimizations, such as sexual abuse, physical abuse, bullying, and exposure to family violence. The definition emphasizes experiencing different kinds of victimization, rather than multiple episodes of the same kind of victimization. *Children's Exposure to Violence: A Comprehensive National Survey.* Finkelhor, D., Turner, H., Ormrod, R., Hamby S. & Kracke, K. U.S. Department of Justice, Office of Juvenile Justice and Delinquency Programs. (2009).

[35] *2012 Trafficking in Persons Report*, U.S. Department of State.

[36] *Addressing the Needs of Victims of Human Trafficking: Challenges, Barriers, and Promising Practices.* Heather J. Clawson and Nicole Dutch, Aug. 2008.

PHOTO CREDITS: